ZONING, RENT CONTROL and AFFORDABLE HOUSING

ZONING, RENT CONTROL and AFFORDABLE HOUSING

WILLIAM TUCKER

CATO INSTITUTE
Washington D.C.

Library of Congress Cataloging-in-Publication Data

Tucker, William, 1942-
    Zoning, rent control, and affordable housing / by William
Tucker.
    p.   cm.
    Includes bibliographical references.
    ISBN 0-932790-78-X : $9.95
    1. Housing policy—United States. 2. Municipal government—
United States. 3. Zoning, Exclusionary—United States. 4. Rent
control—United States.   5. Public Housing—United
States.   6. Poor—Housing—United States. I. Title.
HD7293.T774 1991
363.5'56'0973—dc20   91-29205
                                          CIP

Contents

1. Introduction

> In New York City, a welfare family spends its last $600 to make the security deposit on a scarce apartment in the Bedford-Stuyvesant district. When they show up the next day, they find it is a scam. The "rental agent" has collected a $600 deposit for the same apartment from six other desperate people. The family spends Christmas homeless.
>
> In Santa Monica, California, Michael Kann, columnist for the *Los Angeles Herald Examiner*, spent several years writing *Middle Class Radicalism in Santa Monica*, a book that praised the city's rent control. Still, he was forced to note, "I know one professional woman who tried to get a Santa Monica apartment for more than a year without success, but she broke into the city, finally, by marrying someone who already had an apartment there."
>
> In Berkeley, California, hordes of homeless people crowd into a meeting of the city council to complain about their plight. The meeting becomes so rowdy that even Mayor Loni Hancock, of the radical Berkeley Citizens' Action party, who is sympathetic to the homeless, gavels for quiet. "All right, if we can't have order here, I'm going to end the meeting and send everyone home," she shouts above the din. "How can you do that?" replies one homeless man. "We don't have a home."

As the 1980s drew to a close, Americans found themselves living in the midst of a "housing crisis." Every winter the newspapers carried pathetic stories of elderly bag ladies and parents with children roaming the streets without a place to live. The "lack of affordable housing" was perceived as a national issue for which the social service cutbacks by the Reagan administration were commonly held responsible.

The most frequently cited figure was the reduction in the Department of Housing and Urban Development's spending authorization, which fell from $31 billion in 1980 to only $7 billion in 1988. "The Federal government hasn't just walked away from its role in

1

the housing market, it has run away," said former New York mayor Edward Koch. "The consequences have been disastrous."[1]

Yet the supposedly national housing crisis had some puzzling aspects. The rising problem of homelessness, plus the general complaints about lack of affordable housing, seemed to suggest that rental housing was in short supply. Yet the truth was just the opposite. Rental vacancies, at a healthy 6 percent at the start of the decade, had risen to a 25-year high of 7.8 percent by 1989. Even the elimination of tax incentives for the construction of rental housing in the Tax Reform Act of 1986 did not put a dent in the broad availability of rental housing.

Moreover, if there was a genuine housing crisis in some parts of the country, it was a problem of too much housing. Houston, Dallas, Phoenix, and New Orleans were swamped with vacancies. In Phoenix, developers were giving away two months' free rent in an attempt to persuade people to sign a one-year lease. During the 1988 presidential campaign, there was frequent mention of Republican candidate George Bush's investment in a "troubled Houston apartment complex." The trouble with the complex—as with so many others in Houston—was that no tenants could be found to live in it. Vacancy rates in Houston were an astonishing 18 percent—more than twice the national average and almost 10 times the rates in cities such as New York and San Francisco.

What was going on? Why were vacancy rates astronomically high in some cities and microscopically small in others? Why were homeless populations so unevenly distributed? As June Q. Koch of the U.S. Department of Housing and Urban Development noted:

> HUD found wide variations in the size and nature of the homeless population from region to region and from city to city. The highest concentration of homeless was found in the West, which has only 19 percent of the nation's population but almost one-third of all homeless people in metropolitan areas. By way of contrast, the South, with 33 percent of the total national population, has only 24 percent of the homeless population.[2]

[1]Remarks by Mayor Edward I. Koch at the housing-capital funds press conference, April 30, 1986.

[2]June Q. Koch, "The Federal Role in Aiding the Homeless," in *The Homeless in Contemporary Society*, ed. Richard D. Bingham, Roy E. Green, and Sammis B. White (Newbury Park, Calif.: Sage Publications, 1987), p. 218.

That pattern is the opposite of the normal perception of the nation's distribution of wealth. In general, the South is perceived as somewhat backward economically, whereas the Far West, if it has not quite yet matched the Northeast in concentrated wealth and income, is seen as by far the most rapidly expanding and newly prosperous region. However, when it comes to homelessness and shortages of affordable housing, the South does not do nearly as badly as the Far West.

What is the explanation? In 1987, in search of an answer, I compiled figures on per capita homelessness in 50 cities, using mostly a 1984 report to the secretary of housing and urban development on homelessness and temporary shelters.[3] Using multiple regression analysis, I sought correlations between high rates of homelessness and a dozen factors that have been suggested as contributing to the problem. A summary of the results is given in Table 1–1.

Table 1–1
POSSIBLE CAUSES OF HOMELESSNESS

Variable	R^2	P
Median home price	42	<.001
Rent control	26	<.001
Rental vacancy rate	15	<.005
Minority population	11	.021
Median rent	8	.052
Poverty rate	5	.107
Average annual temperature	3	.177
Public housing per capita	2	.282
Unemployment rate	1	.406
Size of city	1	.459
Percentage of growth over last 15 years	1	.450
Average annual rainfall	0	.986

Note: R^2 expresses the percentage of change in the dependent variable that can be associated with a change in the independent variable.

P is a measure of the certainty of the correlation. P generally has to be less than .1 to be considered statistically significant.

[3]*A Report to the Secretary on the Homeless and Emergency Shelters* (Washington: U.S. Department of Housing and Urban Development, 1984).

As can be seen in Table 1-1, 42 percent of the variation in the homeless population of the 50 cities correlates with variations in the median price of homes. Only 1 percent of the variation in homelessness can be associated with differences in unemployment rates among the cities. Five variables—median home price, presence of rent control, rental vacancy rate, size of the minority population, and median rent—show statistical significance. P-values in the top two correlations—median home price and the presence of rent control—show almost absolute statistical certainty.

The statistics suggest that poverty, unemployment, and lack of public housing—factors often cited as causes of homelessness—do not correlate significantly with high homeless populations. What is significant is the availability of housing in the private market. The presence of a large minority population also makes a small difference—correlating with 11 percent of the variation. That may not be surprising, since all surveys of homeless populations are now reporting a sizable overrepresentation of minority groups.

Yet by far the most significant factor is the availability of private housing. Median rent makes a small difference; higher rents correlate with more homelessness. Vacancy rates make an even bigger difference; cities with low vacancy rates have significantly more homeless people. Rent control makes an enormous difference. The simple presence of rent control produces 2.5 times more homelessness in any city than it would otherwise experience. Moreover, when the different variables were run together, the vacancy factor essentially dropped out and only the presence of rent control made a difference. The nine rent-controlled cities had the nine lowest vacancy rates in the country. Only one city without rent control (Worcester, Massachusetts) had a vacancy rate under 4 percent, and no rent-controlled city had a vacancy rate over 3 percent.[4]

The significant correlation between the median price of homes and the rate of homelessness also reinforces the suggestion that the private market is the key to understanding homelessness. What has pushed up the price of homes in certain metropolitan regions but not others? Is it a high demand for housing? Is it a lack of

---

[4]For a more detailed account of the regression analysis, see William Tucker, *The Excluded Americans: Homelessness and Housing Policies* (Washington: Regnery Gateway, 1990), chap. 3.

4

supply? And if supplies are at fault, what is causing the lack thereof? Zoning efforts and "growth controls" are obvious suspects.

Even more interesting is the very close correlation between metropolitan regions with high housing prices and cities with rent control. Are the two interrelated? If so, how?

Homeownership and pressures on the rental market are closely related. People who rent are usually young and relatively poor. As their incomes rise, they move up to homeownership, encouraged by the long-term investment, the deductibility of mortgage interest from their income taxes, and the general satisfactions that go with owning one's own home.

In a market characterized by high home prices, however, young people may not be able to move up to homeownership. They are forced to remain in the rental market where they compete with people poorer than themselves, thereby driving up rents.

That would not necessarily cause a housing shortage, since the pressure on rents would cause developers to build more housing, bringing rents down again. But what if a city doesn't let that happen? What if it imposes rent controls or growth-control measures? As we shall see, that has been a common pattern in the cities that now have high rates of homelessness.

Communities in the San Francisco area, for example, enacted a wave of no-growth ordinances and tightened zoning restrictions in the 1970s. Then, in 1979, a string of Bay Area communities—San Francisco, Oakland, Berkeley, and San Jose—adopted rent control. Regulation-happy Berkeley is even talking about putting price controls on the sale of single-family homes. In 1970 home prices in the Bay Area were no higher than the national average. Today they are twice the national average and the highest in the country. Altogether, the region has the highest housing prices, the lowest rental vacancy rates, and one of the largest homeless populations in the nation.

Just which of those actions is cause and which is effect is difficult to say. But one thing is obvious: Stringent housing regulations have certainly not helped the San Francisco area solve its housing problems. They may even be creating the problems.

Let us take a closer look at the Bay Area to see how its purported housing crisis has evolved.

2. Welcome to California

In 1978 the Santa Cruz City Council adopted a new zoning requirement for houses built in the foothills surrounding that oceanside community. The council's concern was a species of salamander that lived in the hills but migrated once a year to a series of lakes at the bottom of the valley. To preserve the salamanders' mating habits, all new homes would have to be built on stilts, with an elaborate series of ramps and passageways to ensure the salamanders' progress through the residential districts.

In 1982 Marty Schiffenbauer, the original architect of Berkeley's draconican rent-control ordinance, told Berkeley's affluent academic community that rent control had afforded them the opportunity to move spending out of housing and into other consumer tastes. "The next time you're drinking Perrier or dining at [an expensive Berkeley restaurant], you can thank rent control," he said.

In 1989 Redwood City removed a three-year building moratorium and allowed the construction of new homes. Shortly afterward, a group of anonymous vigilantes took matters into their own hands. Over a period of two weeks, they set fire to more than 20 new homes that were being constructed in the small South San Francisco Bay community, doing $2 million in damage. Mike Martin, arson investigator for the California Department of Forestry, said he suspected anti-growth sentiment.

Despite a slowdown since the 1960s, California remains the fastest growing state in the country. One-fourth of the population growth in the United States occurs in California, and the state now has the eighth largest economy in the world.

Few people would accuse Californians of refusing to accept growth. Still, during the 1970s and 1980s the state was growing much faster than most people wanted. Concerned about the loss of environmental amenities, solitude, and the quality of life, Californians up and down the coast tightened zoning ordinances and adopted growth moratoria, trying to keep out further development. Discovering a group of refugees from Los Angeles and San Francisco trying to draw the line again in rural Sonoma County, *Newsweek* reported:

> Newcomers arrive with lots of equity from selling overpriced homes elsewhere. They drive up housing costs and build pseudo-French mansions with hot tubs and sprawling decks. They clog the roads. Anxious to protect their land from people just like themselves, the jealous pioneers of the new California dream outlaw development once they're settled, trying hard to close the door behind them.[1]

Although suburban resistance to new growth was well documented, and often widely praised, few people were willing to calculate how that resistance related to another social problem, the so-called housing crisis. Those who did found that controlling growth had one obvious result—higher housing prices.

After carefully surveying the developments of the last two decades in California, Lawrence Katz and Kenneth Rosen, of the Institute of Business and Economic Research at the University of California, Berkeley, discovered that until 1970 housing prices in California had been in line with the national average. Thereafter, prices in California as a whole, and in the San Francisco and Los Angeles areas in particular, climbed to more than double the national average. Katz and Rosen attributed the increase to (1) an upsurge in migration, (2) a surge in household formations by the baby-boom generation, and (3) "a massive increase in the use of land-use and growth management techniques to slow and stop new housing production."[2]

In particular, the authors noted that farmland—the land most commonly used for new development—was not particularly expensive in California and notably cheaper than in many areas of the country (Table 2–1).

[1]"California: American Dream, American Nightmare," *Newsweek*, July 31, 1989, p. 29.

[2]Lawrence Katz and Kenneth T. Rosen, "The Effects of Land-Use Controls on Housing Prices" (Institute of Business and Economic Research, Berkeley, Calif., 1980.)

8

Table 2-1
LAND PRICES

State	Average Cost of Farmland per Acre ($)	Average Cost of Building Lot ($)
California	844	28,466
Florida	838	12,049
Illinois	1,484	16,484
Michigan	708	12,986
New Jersey	1,884	16,486

"The high cost of developed lots in California is not caused by the high price of rural farm land. . . . In our view, the main explanation . . . is local land-use regulations," concluded Katz and Rosen.[3]

In particular, they pointed to the effects of exclusionary zoning policies, large-lot requirements, impact fees that often load community costs on new developments, and growth moratoria that prohibit new development outright. Using linear regressions, the authors compared the effects of land-use regulations on housing prices in a number of northern California communities. They concluded that "a community with growth moratoria in effect for more than two years will have house prices [$20,000 to $30,000] higher than a comparable nonmoratoria community."[4]

High housing prices in both the Los Angeles and the San Francisco areas, then, have largely been the result of rising demand pushing against a market that has been severely restricted by the unwillingness of current residents to allow new housing to be built. That resistance has been expressed through municipal intervention in the housing market—zoning restrictions, growth controls, and moratoria on new construction.

Yet municipal intervention should not necessarily produce a housing shortage. Suburbs, after all, are a relatively recent American invention. Previously, both rich and poor people lived in major cities. At the turn of the 19th century, most American cities were packed to far greater densities than they are today. If preserving the rural environment, or someone's suburban amenities, is judged

[3]Ibid., pp. 41–42.
[4]Ibid., p. 45.

9

an acceptable social goal, then cities could probably accommodate more people.

Alas, the cities—many of the most important ones at least—have also been resisting growth. San Francisco is a notable example. Obsessed with the notion that it was ruining its skyline, the city began putting height restrictions on new buildings in the 1970s. Then, in 1984, it came up with the most ambitious program in American history for controlling downtown development. The city set a quota that allows the equivalent of only one large new office building to be built each year. Developers submit architectural plans when they bid for the new construction. The idea is to turn the bidding process into a method of improving the city's skyline by giving planners control over the design of new development.

Even in its own terms, the controlled-growth scheme has been a complete failure. Billed as an effort to apply "good planning methods" to urban development, it has instead brought forth a trickle of buildings that one architectural critic calls "tame, even dull."[5] Instead of submitting bold designs—the kind that might produce another Transamerica building, which now dominates the city's skyline—developers have proposed stolid, unimaginative rectangular designs in hopes of finding the lowest common denominator among the judges.

Office construction does not produce housing, of course, but it does express a city's receptivity to development in general. Not surprisingly, San Francisco has the same slow-growth attitude toward new residential construction it does toward new office buildings—with the same results. New apartment buildings are so scarce in San Francisco—and subjected to such a maze of regulatory review—that they are commonly filled two years before they open.

To try to compensate for its obviously restrictive no-growth policies, San Francisco has chosen two policy courses that have been repeated around the country. It has (1) imposed rent control and (2) initiated "inclusionary zoning" policies.

Rent control came to San Francisco almost by accident—as is often the case with rent-control ordinances. Faced with a wave of price inflation in the late 1970s—as was the rest of the country—

---

[5]Paul Goldberger, "For San Francisco, 'Cure' Is Worse Than High-Rise 'Disease,'" *New York Times*, December 5, 1987.

San Francisco imposed a six-month temporary freeze on rents in 1979. Once in place, the ordinance proved difficult to undo. It was extended several times and finally made permanent in 1982.

The pathological effects of rent control on a housing market are so pervasive—and so utterly predictable—that it will be worthwhile to devote a whole chapter to them (see Chapter 7). For now, however, let us look at the other strategy that San Francisco and hundreds of other communities have used to try to offset the results of their regulatory practices—inclusionary zoning.

Inclusionary zoning, billed as a way of providing "affordable" housing, is an outgrowth of exclusionary zoning, which generally makes housing more unaffordable. When zoning was first introduced in New York City in 1915, it was advertised as a method of keeping undesired industrial and commercial uses out of residential areas. Zoning officials would carefully plan communities to keep industrial, commercial, and residential uses in their proper places.

In the suburbs it has become common practice to exclude nearly all land uses except single-family homes—and even single-family homes are regarded as less preferable than open space. Apartment houses, two-family homes, triplexes, fourplexes, mobile homes—anything that smacks of "low-income housing"—are routinely excluded on the grounds that there is no land within the community where those types of construction are deemed "proper uses of land." Industrial and commercial buildings are tolerated only to the degree that they are "clean ratables"—nonnoxious uses that will pay large portions of the property tax bill.

What the proponents of zoning never seem to recognize, of course, is that separation of land uses would occur without zoning. Houston has absolutely no zoning restrictions, yet it has hardly turned into a massive municipal slum. Deed restrictions on residential property keep gas stations and junkyards out of residential neighborhoods. (Banks will not loan money on developments that do not have such deed restrictions.) Exclusion-minded residents can keep unwanted uses out of their own neighborhood, but they cannot impose restrictions on other neighborhoods six blocks away—or on the other side of town. Thus, Houston has developed both highly exclusive, upper-income neighborhoods *and* low-income neighborhoods that together have created the country's most vibrant housing market and given the city a rate of homelessness that does not exceed the national median.

Inclusionary zoning, on the other hand, is an attempt to compensate for the adverse effects of exclusionary zoning by allowing a little trickle of low-income housing that will supposedly offset the general restrictions on the housing market.

Typically, a builder is awarded a "density bonus" that allows him to add extra apartments to a new residential complex if he rents those units to people with low to moderate incomes. In San Francisco, inclusionary zoning has been expanded so that developers of office complexes are also required to construct inclusionary units. The problem is that inclusionary units rarely are occupied by the poor.

A pricing system, after all, is a system of rationing. People acquire things according to how much money they can afford to spend. True, poor people often can afford very little, but in most cases they can afford something. The whole idea of an apartment house is to allow people who are poorer than homeowners to acquire housing by settling for less space and less access to the outdoors. In the eyes of suburban homeowners, an apartment may be a poor substitute for good housing, but it may be all the less affluent can afford.

For inclusionary housing, however, the primary rationing mechanism is information, not income. Apartments are offered at below-market prices. Since their low price makes them attractive to many more people than would rent them on the open market, income does not work as a means of rationing. Sometimes lotteries are held; sometimes select groups like municipal employees or senior citizens are given preference. But for the most part, distribution is first-come, first-served. That means that people who are more alert to the allotment process—or who even have access to inside information—get first choice. Interestingly enough, affluent people often find their buying power enhanced by an information-rationing system.

According to a report that appeared in 1989 in the *San Francisco Chronicle:*

> Despite a citywide shortage of cheap apartments, one in six units set aside for low-income San Franciscans is sitting vacant in six snazzy new renewal projects, a new report [by the San Francisco Redevelopment Agency] shows. . . .
> All six projects were built in redevelopment areas by private developers who received federal tax breaks by agreeing

to set aside a fifth of their units for low-and-moderate income tenants. . . .

Housing advocates have long complained that the developers have geared their projects to young professionals and affluent singles with advertisements promoting a resort-like lifestyle. . . .

The redevelopment study found that 15 of the 86 units are unoccupied. . . . Of those that are occupied, 90 percent of the tenants are white.[6]

Although that case obviously hinged on the desire of a private developer not to spoil the residential ambience designed for young professionals, the same pattern has occurred everywhere inclusionary zoning has been practiced.

In New Jersey inclusionary zoning is being used to implement the court's decision in the Mt. Laurel zoning case, which was brought to break down zoning barriers to the poor. Yet the results have been the same. The *New York Times* reported:

The first trickle of affordable homes . . . has not gone to the inner-city poor [who,] with their meager incomes and weak credit ratings, . . . either cannot qualify for or afford a down-payment.

Instead, the homes, generally priced between $20,000 and $70,000, have been snapped up by others who qualify as low- and moderate-income buyers, most notably young professional families and divorced, single, and retired people.[7]

In Island Trees, Long Island, the home town of Sen. Alfonse D'Amato (R-N.Y.), several friends and relations of public officials (including one of the senator's relatives) were able to secure housing that was supposedly intended for the poor. They slipped their applications under the door of the town clerk's office on the very morning an obscure notice advertising for applicants appeared in the newspapers. All had been privy to inside information.

Thus, inclusionary zoning ordinances designed to create "affordable housing" have instead created a system whereby established

[6]Steve Massey, "Vacancies in S.F. Renewal Projects," *San Francisco Chronicle*, August 16, 1989, p. A9.

[7]Robert Hanley, "Affordable Housing in Jersey Is Still an Elusive Goal," *New York Times*, October 24, 1988, p. B1.

13

residents of an exclusion-minded community can limit housing construction while providing subsidized housing to knowledgeable insiders—all under the pretense of helping the poor. It is no surprise that cities such as San Francisco and Boston that have tried to compensate for exclusionary practices with inclusionary requirements have ended up with large homeless populations.

3. The Mechanics of Rent Control

When it comes to excluding outsiders and creating havoc at the lower end of a housing market, nothing matches the power of rent control.

Rent control is part of a larger schema known to economists as price controls. The common perception of price controls is that they make commodities and services cheap and plentiful. All that is necessary is to lower their prices. Often price controls have been imposed on an entire economy in an effort to stop inflation. At other times, only certain commodities have been singled out. In 1980, for example, Sen. Edward Kennedy ran for president on a platform that included a call for controlling inflation by imposing price controls on major materials, energy, and medical services.

For about a century, economists have understood in clear mathematical terms why price controls do not work. (Adam Smith and other economists understood the problem in broad, logical categories but did not reduce it to mathematical theory.) The pioneering work was done by British economist Alfred Marshall, who in the 1890s formulated what are known as the laws of supply and demand.

The laws of supply and demand can be expressed in a simple graph (Figure 3–1) that plots the behavior of both producers and consumers over a range of price options. The horizontal axis represents the number of transactions desired by consumers and producers. The vertical axis represents a price range over which those transactions may occur. Thus, the various points on the graph represent the number of desired transactions at any given price.

The desires of consumers and producers are different, of course, so each is represented by a separate curve. The supply curve, representing the behavior of sellers, runs upward to the right, indicating that as the price of a given commodity rises, suppliers want to sell more of it. The demand curve runs in the opposite direction, indicating, quite logically, that as prices rise, consumers buy less and, as prices fall, they want to buy more.

Figure 3–1
SUPPLY AND DEMAND

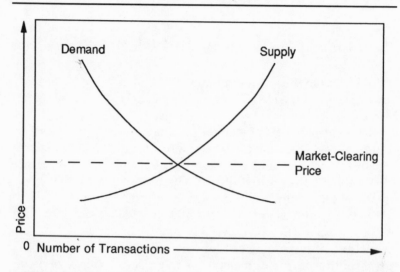

Thus, it might seem that the desires of consumers and producers are irreconcilably opposed. One group wants higher prices and the other wants lower. What is important, however, is that at one point the two curves intersect. That intersection—where the desires of both buyers and sellers are brought into alignment—is called the equilibrium, or market-clearing, price.

The market price is set by the desires of both consumers and producers. Neither dictates a price to the other. There will always be fewer producers than consumers, since that is the nature of the division of labor. Individual consumers may feel overshadowed by big producers, but those very producers feel equally intimidated by the buying public, over which they have no control. Neither is ever completely satisfied. Producers will always want to see prices a little higher, and consumers will want them lower. Yet there will always be a point at which they agree—the market-clearing price.

In *The Evolution of Cooperation*, Robert Axelrod used a simple game called Prisoners' Dilemma to explore the nature of that kind of voluntary cooperation.[1] In the game, two players win points by cooperating with each other. Each can win a greater number of

[1]Robert Axelrod, *The Evolution of Cooperation* (New York: Basic Books, 1984).

points by successfully betraying the other player and refusing to cooperate, but if both players try to betray the other, they get nowhere.

Axelrod found that graduate students assigned to play the game continually expressed frustration at not being able to control the other player's actions. Buyers and sellers in the marketplace face the same problem. Each must win the cooperation of the other if a transaction is to take place. Yet neither party can dictate the terms of the transaction. Instead, both parties must find a common ground on which they can agree.

Players are always tempted, however, to find some third party or superior force to compel the other player to accept their terms. Price supports or price control are the result of those impulses.

Price supports come into being when producers are able to persuade the government (a third party) to raise prices above their market value. That is usually done on the pretext that there is some special quality about a product that makes it essential to keep more producers in the market. Farmers in Europe, America, and Japan, for example, have long been granted price supports on the grounds that every country needs indigenous food production. (In the Third World, on the other hand, urban majorities usually force the government to impose price controls on food on the grounds that the country's most important task is to feed its urban masses.) The outcome is shown in Figure 3–2.

The supply and demand curves are unchanged, but now the government has arbitrarily imposed a price that is above the market-clearing price. Two things happen as a result. Producers, seeing a higher price, move outward on the supply curve and bring more goods to market. They grow more corn, or add more cows to their herds, in the expectation of reaping a greater profit. Consumers, on the other hand, see a higher price and move back on the demand curve. They now buy less because they don't like the higher price. The result is an excess of supply over demand, or what is called an economic surplus—such as a "farm surplus."

Despite a few obvious cases such as agricultural supports or government-fixed stockbrokers' fees, price supports are rare. That is because the division of labor always puts consumers in the majority. As a result it is far easier for the consuming majority to use its overwhelming political numbers to strong-arm the government into controlling prices. The results are shown in Figure 3–3.

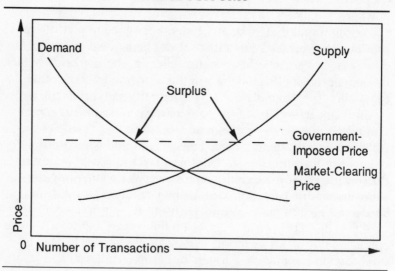

Figure 3–2
PRICE SUPPORTS

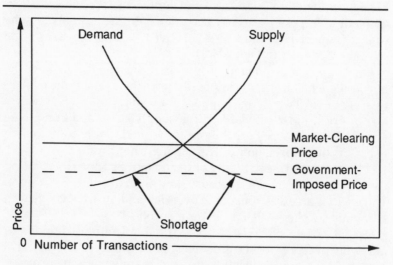

Figure 3–3
EFFECT OF PRICE CONTROLS

Now it is consumers, attracted by the low prices, who want more transactions. But producers, discouraged by the new low price, do not bring as many products to market. Once again a gap opens between supply and demand. That gap is called an economic shortage.

The oil shortages of the 1970s were the result of price controls. Oil prices were first controlled in 1971, under President Richard Nixon's general wage and price controls, and not lifted until President Ronald Reagan's first week in office in 1981. During much of that time, the effect of price controls was obscured by the Arab oil boycott and other international events. Yet the basic problem of the era was an economic shortage of domestic oil created by federal price controls. As U.S. oil supplies ran short, we went abroad to make up for the shortage. That made us vulnerable to even the slightest disturbances in foreign supplies. (The Iranian revolution of 1979 cut international supplies only 4 percent.) When price controls were removed in 1981, domestic supply and demand were brought back into line and the problem solved itself.

The example of the oil shortages of the 1970s points to an important lesson about price controls. Both producers and consumers—and even the government itself—will try very hard to get around the inevitable shortage of the controlled commodity by conjuring up an unregulated sector or a black market. Prices in the unregulated sector or black market will actually be higher than they would be without the regulations. That is because the excess demand left over from the regulated market will be matched against the limited supplies in the unregulated or black market.

Thus, the remarkably high prices of foreign oil in the 1970s were actually the result of U.S. domestic price controls. Price controls created unsatisfied domestic demand that had to be satisfied from abroad. Soon after price controls on U.S. oil were removed, the price of foreign oil came tumbling down.

Rent controls—which are simply price controls applied to rental housing—have similar results. Rent controls are now practiced in more than 200 American municipalities. Almost 100 of them are small urban communities in northern New Jersey. The others are large and small cities on the East and West coasts. On the East Coast, Boston, Hartford, Newark, New York, Washington, and most of the population centers on Long Island and in Westchester County now have rent control. On the West Coast, San Francisco, Oakland, San Jose, and Los Angeles, plus smaller cities, such as Berkeley, Santa Monica, North Hollywood, and Palm Springs, also have rent control. More than half the population of California and New York—the two largest states—lives under rent control.

Many of those cities do not exercise rent control very strictly, however. In a 1981 study, the RAND Corporation found that rent control had reduced rents in Los Angeles by only about 2.5 percent. (In contrast, in neighboring Santa Monica, rents have been reduced almost 40 percent.)[2] John I. Gilderbloom and Richard P. Appelbaum, two supporters of rent control, have complained that there is no evidence that rent control, as practiced in many New Jersey municipalities, reduces rents at all.[3]

Proponents of rent control often try to distinguish between moderate and severe ordinances, arguing that moderate rent control can be tolerated because it avoids the obvious bad effects of severe rent control. Yet the underlying principle is the same. If a city has moderate rent control, it will have a moderate housing shortage; if it has severe rent control, it will have a severe housing shortage. Moreover, once in place, rent controls are likely to gain a momentum of their own. Almost all the nation's rent-control ordinances started as temporary measures intended to deal with inflation, not a housing crisis. The housing crisis came later. Unfortunately, the more rent control a city has, the worse the housing crisis becomes, and the worse the housing crisis becomes, the more people demand that rent control be expanded and enforced more severely.

In practice, how does a shortage of housing develop under rent control? First, builders are likely to stop putting up new housing because they see their future profits being captured by rent control. New housing starts have all but ceased in cities with strict rent control. In 1987 San Francisco, with a vacancy rate of 1.8 percent, added only 2,000 new units to its housing supply, whereas Dallas, with a vacancy rate of 13 percent, added 12,000.

Second, landlords withhold existing housing from the market. That is not as difficult as it may sound. One-quarter of the housing market is single-family homes, and another quarter is small buildings with only two to four rental units. Landlords can easily reclaim those units for owner occupancy or for use by friends and relatives.

[2]C. Peter Rydell et al., *The Impact of Rent Control on the Los Angeles Housing Market* (Santa Monica, Calif.: RAND Corporation, 1981).

[3]John I. Gilderbloom and Richard P. Appelbaum, *Rethinking Rental Housing* (Philadelphia: Temple University Press, 1988).

In Toronto, which has very strict rent control, 23 percent of all rental units in owner-occupied dwellings were withdrawn from the market within three years of the imposition of rent control in 1976. The result was a 12 percent reduction in rental housing stock.[4]

On the demand side, consumers start trying to "overconsume" by staying in apartments that are either too small or too large for them. One of the most common effects of rent control is that elderly people stay in large apartments after their children have departed. Conversely, young people may continue to rent when they would ordinarily be moving up to homeownership.

The most common overall effect of rent control is that people simply do not move. Because there is an apartment shortage, it is difficult to find another place to live. In addition, many cities practice "vacancy allowances," which permit landlords to increase rents more when an apartment changes hands. As a result, people who stay in their apartments the longest end up paying rents that are furthest below market. Tenant immobility—sometimes called "housing gridlock"—develops.

In New York City—which has had rent control since 1943—the rate at which people change residences is only one-third the national average. A study conducted by a consulting firm for the Los Angeles Rent Stabilization Division concluded that rent control in that city has basically been an income transfer from people who move often to people who stay put.[5] In Europe, where many countries have had rent control since World War I, "labor immobility" is now regarded as a major barrier to economic progress. Both Great Britain and France are now trying to phase out rent control because they believe they will be unable to compete in a unified Europe if workers remain chained to their rent-controlled apartments.

On the other hand, the housing shortages created by rent control differ in several respects from the shortages produced by price controls on other commodities. The most important difference is the long lifetime of housing and the long period over which people can consume it.

[4]Lawrence B. Smith, "Rent Controls in Ontario: Roofs or Ceilings?" (Institute of Business and Economic Research, Berkeley, Calif., 1981), p. 12.

[5]Hamilton, Rabinovitz, Szanton, and Alschuler, Inc., and the Urban Institute, "Rental Housing Study: The Rent Stabilization System—Impacts and Alternatives" (City of Los Angeles Rent Stabilization Division, April 1985), pp. 32–34.

A person who was renting an apartment in Boston in 1971 when rent control was imposed may still be renting the same apartment today, paying a rent that has drifted 40 to 50 percent below market. Meanwhile, people looking for apartments are either forced into one of the unregulated "holes in the market," where prices are higher than they would be without rent control, or unable to find anything at all.

The usual result of rent control is to split the housing market in two. Some people get great deals while others face housing shortages and higher-than-market prices. Yet strangely enough, the people who suffer the adverse effects rarely blame rent control. Instead, they blame landlords. Or they blame government officials for not enforcing rent control strictly enough. When the sufferers reach a critical mass, politicians are usually forced to respond by tightening or extending rent-control regulations.

Consumers of most other regulated commodities—gasoline, for example—face a more equitably distributed shortfall when price-control–induced shortages occur. When a person buys a tank of gas, he consumes it in about a week and must then go back for another. Thus, hoarding gas is difficult (although John Denver did install two 100-gallon tanks in his front yard during the crisis of 1979). For the most part, though, the pain of the shortage and the rising price on the gray and black markets during an oil shortage are experienced by all. Thus, it is easier to get rid of other types of price controls than of rent control.

If the results of rent control are so adverse and predictable, why do cities continue to practice it? The answer is illustrated in Figure 3–4.

Bringing down rents by a small amount opens a gap between supply and demand. Half of that gap is really false demand—the desires of people who would not ordinarily be in the market for housing but are attracted by the artificially low prices. The gap to the right of the perpendicular line in Figure 3–4 represents false demand.

The gap to the left of the perpendicular line represents true unsatisfied demand—the demand of the people who are completely closed out of the regulated market by rent control. They must seek more expensive units in the unregulated sector, or may not be able to find anything at all.

Figure 3–4
EFFECTS OF RENT CONTROL

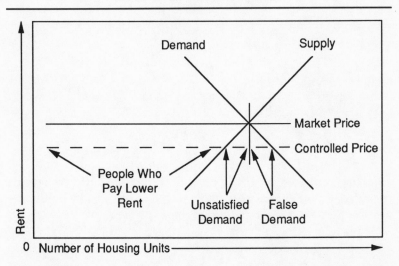

Notice how much greater is the number of people who benefit from rent control than is the number who are penalized. Under rent control most of the tenant population receives a bonus of lower-than-market rents. Only a small percentage of tenants is entirely excluded from the market. That small group must bear *all the adverse consequences.* Those people will be forced out of the market and may even end up homeless. The people who benefit from rent control will always remain the overwhelming majority. That is why rent control may persist—even when housing shortages and increased homelessness are the result.

4. The Liberation of the Professoriate

Berkeley and Santa Monica are two medium-sized cities in California. Both have had rent control since the 1970s. Both practice it with a peculiar ferocity. And both are small enough markets so the effects are diluted very little by other factors. Together, they make an ideal laboratory in which to study rent control in action.

What is worth noting about those cities is that both have a fairly clear-cut demographic profile. Politics in both cities is dominated by a highly educated, affluent, professional upper middle class. That characteristic has been noted by many observers. Anthony Downs of the Brookings Institution noted that "a high proportion of renters" and "a relatively high proportion of college and university students" are the most common traits of rent-controlled communities.[1] Lawrence Friedman, author of *The Government and Slum Housing*, also noted that the reason New York has rent controls while Chicago does not appears to be that New York tenants are more affluent and better educated.[2] Tenants in both Berkeley and Santa Monica are also affluent and well educated.

A second common characteristic of rent control around the country is that it is frequently imposed when a community's population is shifting from manufacturing-oriented people to professional, university-oriented people. Cambridge, Massachusetts, was once a premier manufacturing center. As Harvard and MIT became the dominating economic institutions, Cambridge imposed rent control. In fact, the original petition efforts were initiated in 1969 by two rival left-wing student groups at Harvard in the wake of the Supreme Court's 1968 ruling that students can vote where they attend school. Brookline, Massachusetts, Boston's other suburb

---

[1]Anthony Downs, "Residential Rent Controls: An Evaluation" (Urban Land Institute, Washington, 1988), p. 12.

[2]Lawrence Meir Friedman, *The Government and Slum Housing: A Century of Frustration* (Chicago: Rand McNally and Company, 1968).

with a strong rent-control ordinance, is a community of professional people. Boston itself, of course, is something of a university town.

Berkeley and Santa Monica fit the same pattern. Berkeley instituted rent control shortly after the Supreme Court ruling, which left the University of California's 30,000 students in virtual control of the city's politics. Santa Monica adopted rent control after the formerly sleepy seaside resort—whose main employer was a neighboring Curtiss-Wright plant—was invaded by upscale professionals who migrated westward along the new Santa Monica Freeway. As Richard Devine noted in an extensive study of the two communities, Berkeley and Santa Monica have the highest percentages of college-oriented professionals of all California cities.[3]

The explanation of the relationship between rent control and relatively wealthy tenants leads right to the heart of the housing problem. The general historical understanding of landlords is that they are a wealthy group—even a landed aristocracy—that lives in relative idleness by collecting rent from the poor. Books on tenant movements casually liken contemporary renters to medieval tenant farmers, and enthusiasts of rent control such as Gilderbloom and Appelbaum speak of the "deep-seated historical antipathy to landlording."[4]

What few people seem to realize is that landlording has undergone a historic transformation in this country; it is no longer the province of the upper classes. Landlords are now primarily members of the "working" classes—people who entered the field through the building trades or who bought rental property as a part-time investment or as a vehicle for upward mobility or retirement security. As Anthony Downs writes:

> Reliable data on who owns the nation's rental housing are not available, but my impression is that ownership is scattered among many small-scale landlords. This impression is based on the high percentage of rental housing containing fewer than five units, and on my experience in talking to realtors and investors across the nation over the past fifteen years. Many large-scale real estate investors avoid

[3]Richard J. Devine, "Who Benefits from Rent Control?" (Center for Community Change, Oakland, Calif., 1986).

[4]John I. Gilderbloom and Richard P. Appelbaum, *Rethinking Rental Housing* (Philadelphia: Temple University Press, 1988), p. 128.

residential properties, primarily because the high tenant turnover . . . raises management costs . . . compared with other rental real estate.[5]

In fact, the widespread ownership of rental housing has been documented far better than Downs suggests. Studies in the smallest towns and biggest cities have shown that rarely if ever does the biggest landlord own more than 4 to 5 percent of the rental market. In a survey of 700 New York City landlords, Arthur D. Little, Inc., found that 60 percent of New York's landlords own one building and that the median holding is about 10 rental units (an average-sized building by New York standards).[6] New York's largest landlord is the city of New York itself, which owns 9 percent of the market, having acquired tens of thousands of apartments from bankrupt landlords as a result of rent control. The largest private owner—Harry Helmsley—owned only 3 percent in 1986, when he began dissolving his holdings because of the frustrations of dealing with rent control.

The building trades have long been a point of entry for landlording. Landlords tend to be carpenters, plumbers, electricians, and other small investors. The relatively limited capital and minimal skills required for entry are what make ownership of rental housing attractive to amateurs. The skills, after all, are basically janitorial. Many landlords buy otherwise unpromising buildings on the assumption that they will save money by being their own superintendents and doing most of the maintenance and repair work themselves. As Downs writes:

> Small-scale investors who manage their own properties rarely take full account of the cost of their time, so they have lower management costs . . . than large-scale operators who employ professional management and maintenance personnel. That often leads small-scale operators to charge lower rents than those needed by large-scale operators to earn yields competitive with alternative investments.[7]

[5]Anthony Downs, *Rental Housing in the 1980s* (Washington: Brookings Institution, 1984), p. 35.

[6]Arthur D. Little, Inc., "The Owners of New York's Rental Housing: A Profile" (Arthur D. Little, Cambridge, Mass., May 1985), pp. 2–5.

[7]Ibid., p. 34.

The pattern of small-scale ownership has been verified by every major study that has been done on ownership of rental housing. In 1966 George Sternlieb of Rutgers University studied ownership patterns in Newark, New Jersey, and published his findings in *The Tenement Landlord*. Sternlieb found that rental ownership was completely dominated by small operators. "Craftsmen"—both factory workers and household craftsmen—were the largest occupational group, making up 31 percent of all owners. People who listed their profession as "retired" were second, with 13 percent. (Two landlords listed their profession as "unemployed.") Lawyers, the traditional "slumlords," accounted for only 5 percent of owners, and big businessmen only 1 percent. "Housewives" accounted for 4 percent.[8]

Of course, Sternlieb was surveying the tenement districts of Newark, and his findings do not reflect a nationwide pattern. But the general point holds true: most landlords are of the same economic stratum as their tenants. Landlords may generally be a little more affluent than their tenants, although often they are notably less affluent. In general, wealthy tenants have wealthy landlords, middle-class tenants have middle-class landlords, and poor tenants have poor landlords. Thus, it might seem that we should expect an even distribution of landlords—until we remember that tenants are generally the least affluent third of the population. Most people with higher incomes own their own homes.

That explains why rent control has been so common in communities that have undergone a transformation from a manufacturing base to an upper-middle-class professional or university orientation. The landlords in those towns are generally working people who have saved over the years to buy their buildings—often the ones they live in themselves.

Suddenly, they are overwhelmed by a highly mobile and articulate population of university-oriented professionals who tend to regard their landlords with the same esteem they have for the people who repair their cars. Those professionals are often so young and mobile that even homeownership does not interest them. University students, of course, are the extreme case.

[8]George Sternlieb, *The Tenement Landlord* (New Brunswick, N.J.: Rutgers University Press, 1966), p. 128.

Unfortunately, upper-middle-class professionals usually come equipped with an ideological repertoire that convinces them that they are on the same side with—if not the very embodiment of—the "oppressed classes." Confronting a population of landlords, they imagine that they have at last engaged the enemy. Landlords take large portions of their income without doing any apparent work: They monitor their tenants' behavior (an important part of being a landlord). They often seem to have control over vastly more resources than their dress, demeanor, or level of education should allow—raising the suspicion that there is something "crooked" about them.

And so, with righteousness in their hearts and the elixir of self-interest coursing through their veins, the educated professionals begin to explore rent control.

Improbable though that may seem, it is the only plausible explanation of why rent control has taken root in such bastions of professional and academic success as Cambridge, Brookline, Berkeley, and Santa Monica, while it has been of virtually no interest in working-class towns. Somerville and Lynn, Massachusetts, two working-class suburbs of Boston, adopted rent control in the enthusiasm of the early 1970s, then dropped it. Hayward, Mountain View, Richmond, and dozens of other middle-class suburbs in the San Francisco Bay Area have also rejected rent control. In Palo Alto, a university community that narrowly defeated rent control, the principal opposition came from the NAACP.

As a result, in addition to being communities that now have an acute housing problem, rent-controlled cities such as Berkeley and Santa Monica have become scenes of a peculiarly ugly type of class warfare, in which the educated, affluent, and articulate persecute the uneducated, unaffluent, and inarticulate. The experience of the Floystrups, a Berkeley landlord couple, is typical.

Eva and Ova Floystrup were born in Denmark. Her father was a land-reclamation contractor and his worked for the railroad. When the Nazis invaded Denmark in 1940, they demanded that her father help build airports. When he refused, his business was confiscated. Both families spent much of the war in hiding, fighting in the resistance.

When the war was over, Eva and Ova married and decided to emigrate. "We weren't impoverished over there, but we just wanted to see what the other side of the world was like," says Eva. In 1955 they bought steamship tickets and arrived at the home of relatives in San Francisco with $16.50 in their pockets and their five-year-old daughter in tow. "They paid our first month's rent and gave us two bags of groceries as a housewarming present. From then on, we were on our own," says Eva. Eva and Ova eventually settled in Hayward, a working-class suburb south of Oakland.

In California Ova, who had become a master carpenter under the Danish apprentice system, worked on construction jobs, building houses. After saving for several years, the Floystrups also went into business for themselves. "We would buy a property; my husband would fix it up; and then we would sell it again," says Eva. "I would scout the properties and do the financial work, and my husband would do the carpentry." (As do many men, Ova Floystrup prefers to let his wife do the talking.)

Eventually, they started their own construction business. "We build houses," says Eva proudly. "I find a vacant parcel that looks good, and my husband builds the house from the ground up. He's one of the few people who can take a building from the foundation right up to the roof." Ova has his own crew and subcontracts some of the work, but at age 67 he still spends his days hammering nails. "We're the kind of people who will probably never retire," says Eva, who is 61.

Along the way, around 1965, they picked up two rental buildings on a single piece of property in Berkeley. They rented mostly to undergraduates, a practice that had been common for decades in that college city. (The University of California, with 30,000 enrolled students, provides housing for only 10,000 of them.) The Floystrups collected modest rents and never had any problems with their tenants. Then came rent control.

It began in 1970, shortly after the Supreme Court ruling that college students could vote where they went to school. Two years previous, in 1968, Jerry Rubin had run for mayor of Berkeley in what was widely regarded as a comic protest. By 1971, with the voting age reduced to 18, Berkeley Citizens Action—a radical faction made up entirely of Berkeley graduate students and university-oriented activists—had won control of the city council.

Rent control was passed by referendum in 1971, on the grounds that Berkeley was in the midst of a housing crisis. (The cause of the crisis was probably a new city ordinance that banned all new housing without neighborhood approval. Housing construction had ground to a halt.) The rent-control referendum was challenged in court and eventually overturned in 1976. Another referendum failed in 1978. But in that same election, Howard Jarvis's Proposition 13 was passed—partly on the strength of Jarvis's promise that all California tenants would receive rent reductions. When the rent reductions didn't materialize, California tenants in a dozen cities, including Berkeley, took their revenge by imposing rent control.

The 1979 Berkeley ordinance required that landlords register their property, roll back rents to the 1978 level, and then grant tenants a reduction calibrated to the landlords' property-tax savings from Proposition 13. From that point on, landlords were to be permitted small rent increases at the pleasure of the elected Berkeley Rent Stabilization Board.

As a protest against the ordinance, the Floystrups refused to register their property. "We believe in free enterprise, and we just didn't think it was right," says Eva. In particular, the Floystrups regarded the requirement that they provide a "rent history" to the board as an invasion of their privacy. They did, however, roll back their rents and conform with all the other requirements of the new law. "We wanted to do everything just right so they wouldn't have anything to hold over us," says Eva.

Not all Berkeley landlords managed to do that. Many were confused by the regulations. Others missed a city council resolution of 1980 that declared retroactively that landlords would have to provide documentation for the one-time cost-adjusted rent increase permitted since the original rent-control referendum. That resolution was called Measure I.

As a result, hundreds of Berkeley landlords have fallen into the Measure I trap. In the 1980s, the rent board began encouraging tenants to challenge the legality of their rents, on the basis that landlords might not have documented their 1980 rent increases. When landlords could not provide documentation, all subsequent rent increases were invalidated as well, and landlords were forced to refund "overcharges," which often added up to tens of thousands of dollars. Moreover, if only one apartment is out of compliance, the whole building's rents are judged illegal and refunds must be made to all tenants.

In 1981 the city of Berkeley took the Floystrups to court, charging that all their rents were illegal because they had not properly registered their properties. "We were discussing legal strategy with our attorneys at one point," Eva recalls, "and I said to them, 'I think we should defend ourselves on the Fourth and Fifth Amendments' "— illegal search and exemption from self-incrimination. "Our lawyers laughed, but the next day they came back and said, 'We're not going to use the Fourth, but we're going to try the Fifth.' "

In a preliminary hearing, an Alameda County Superior Court judge ruled that the Floystrups could challenge the registration requirements on Fifth Amendment grounds. At the same time, the judge proposed a compromise whereby the Floystrups could pay their $12-per-apartment registration fees (which the city was refusing to accept) and legally register their property without submitting all the rent-history information. That would make the Floystrups' rents legal, pending the outcome of the trial. Both the Floystrups and the city of Berkeley signed a stipulation accepting the compromise.

Within a few months, the city began to have second thoughts about going to trial with the case. City attorneys apparently didn't feel comfortable defending Berkeley's ordinance against the Floystrups' Fifth Amendment challenge. Rather than risk the entire city ordinance, Berkeley officials decided to drop the case in 1982. As a result, the written stipulation signed by both parties became a permanent arrangement. The Floystrups were now legally registered. Yet they remained a thorn in the city's side, openly defying the rent-history requirement.

Over the next five years, the Floystrups noticed a distinct change in the behavior of their tenants. "We used to rent to undergraduates for a few years and then they'd be gone," says Eva. "But once rent control came, the same ones stayed on and on. They just sit there forever, like barnacles."

The Floystrups' tenants were all typical Berkeley students—an architect, a lawyer, a school teacher, a Ph.D. candidate. Many had already begun their graduate work when rent control arrived and had since moved into various professions. Some were now in their mid-30s, but they still hung on to their student apartments. In 1987 they were paying rents of $320 to $390—probably half the market price.

"They all think they're so smart because they're living on such cheap rent," says Eva. "What they don't realize is they're missing all the appreciation they could get by buying a house. Then the new undergraduates come around to me and say, 'How come I can't find an apartment in Berkeley?' I tell them, 'You want an apartment? You'll have to vote against rent control. We're still taking care of the Class of '79.' "

Since the Floystrups and their tenants knew each other well, none of them questioned the stipulation agreement. The city of Berkeley, however, did try to challenge it—even though the city was a party to the stipulation. Several times, the Rent Stabilization Board sent letters informing the tenants that their building was not legally registered and that they were entitled to large refunds for overcharges. The Floystrups finally went back to court and got a judge to enjoin the city government from soliciting tenants' protests.

Then in December 1986 the Ph.D. candidate married a woman who had been involved in a rent-control campaign in Santa Cruz, another college town on the coast south of San Francisco. She moved into his apartment. Within weeks, she had become apprised of the situation and went to the rent board demanding a refund on the grounds that the Floystrups had never disclosed their rent history. The board ruled that since the city itself had not solicited her complaint, it could be entertained. The city quickly repudiated the court stipulation—which it had signed itself—and ruled that the Floystrups' rents were illegal. Within one month, the board ordered the Floystrups to refund $7,000 to the complaining tenant. The couple was told that they could withhold rent until the restitution was complete.

The new tenant was soon campaigning through the two buildings, telling everyone the Floystrups were "millionaires" who could easily afford to pay refunds to everyone. The other tenants—having known the Floystrups for a decade—initially hesitated about going along. Yet one by one they eventually broke ranks and trekked down to the rent board to collect their refunds. Within six months, the Floystrups had been ordered to pay a total of $71,000 in "illegal overcharges." (Two of the 12 tenants never pressed their cases.) The Floystrups were forced to sell one of their buildings to cover the costs.

"The architect bought a new computer," says Eva; "the woman who started the whole thing bought a new station wagon. Every time I see her drive by I say, 'There goes my car.' Only one tenant used his refund to buy a house. I think he was the only smart one." The rent board also rolled back everyone's rents to 1979 levels. The tenants are now paying $190 to $240 for their apartments.

The Floystrups appealed to the Alameda County Superior Court, which had originally approved the stipulation. They were turned down by a new judge. They are now appealing in federal court. Unlike criminal defendants, whose fines are delayed until they have exhausted their appeals, landlords must pay rent refunds while their cases are still pending. The California Supreme Court ruled in 1989 that the requirement for immediate payment violated the state constitution, but the decision came too late to help the Floystrups. Even if they win in court, they will probably never get any money back.

"The thing that surprises me most," Eva says, "is how much the tenants grow to hate you even while you're being forced to provide them with a lifetime subsidy. When that new tenant went before the rent board, she called us the vilest names I ever heard. I told the board, 'Will you please ask her to explain just what these horrible things are that we've been doing to her? We've only had her for a tenant six months and haven't even gotten to know her yet.' She did tell me the building was getting a little shabby. I said I agreed. You only get what you pay for, you know."

Meanwhile, the Floystrups—like many other Berkeley landlords—have found an appealing way to get around rent regulations. They now rent several apartments to recipients of federal section-8 housing vouchers.[9] "I've now managed to get five vacancies, and the section-8 tenants are paying rents between $425 and $615," Eva says. "The government only pays part, but taking a section-8 tenant exempts you from rent control. You'd think if poor people can pay these kinds of rents that middle-class people could be expected to pay a little more, wouldn't you?

[9] Under section 8 of the Housing and Community Development Act of 1974, HUD issues rent certificates that constitute a 15-year commitment by the government to pay the difference between a tenant's rent and 30 percent of his income. Payment is made to the landlord.

"You have to keep a sense of humor about all this," she adds. "My husband and I have worried and spent a few sleepless nights. But every once in a while we look at each other and laugh. We survived the Nazis. We'll survive this."

5. The War between Tenants and Landlords

> One day the landlord will no longer walk the earth. He will
> be as extinct as the feudal lord or the divine right of kings.
> People will react to the idea of being a landlord the way they
> now react to the idea of being a slave trader or a pimp.
> —Letter to the *Berkeley Voice*

If all that happened to a community under rent control were that
it experienced a housing shortage, rent control might be somewhat
bearable. Unfortunately, that is only the beginning. Once rent control becomes embedded in a community's psyche, it produces a
kind of mass insanity that the term "war between tenants and
landlords" only begins to describe.

Do you remember what life was like in the worst moments of the
energy crisis of the late 1970s? Do you remember when truck drivers
were on strike, carrying around signs that read "President Carter,
Kiss My Gas"? Do you remember the quiet terror people felt at the
idea that at any moment the most simple but essential commodity
might not be available? Do you remember how people got out of
bed in the morning and went to bed at night hating the oil companies? Do you remember the stories and rumors—tankers full of oil
sitting offshore waiting for the price to go up? Do you remember
the parade of "energy activists" on television, swearing by all that
is holy that there was plenty of oil in the world and that the greedy
oil companies were deliberately causing a shortage so they could
get a better price?

Well, to a greater or lesser degree, that's what everyday life is
like in a rent-controlled community. Once a community adopts
rent control, the housing issue becomes the predominant factor in
municipal politics. As the *Boston Globe* reported:

> It's not as though the candidates in tomorrow's town
> election haven't had plenty of issues to debate.

37

Parking is in short supply. Small businesses are moving out because of the parking problem and the poor economy. Essential services, including the town's fire and police departments, are threatened in the face of a possible $1.4 million cut in local aid. Schools and other public buildings are in disrepair. Nevertheless, one issue dominates all others in the campaigns for Brookline selectmen and Town Meeting members. It is rent control, the issue that Refuses to Go Away.

"You walk around town as a candidate, and people will say to you, 'Where do you stand on rent control?' " said Linda Fosburg, one of 160 candidates running for 85 open seats in Town Meeting. "It's one of the litmus tests of the town. It's a polarizing force."[1]

How does rent control subsume everything else? First and foremost, rent control requires landlords to subsidize their tenants. Under all other welfare systems, the subsidy is underwritten by the public at large, through taxes. Thus, if the burden becomes too heavy, people are likely to object. But because rent control taxes only landlords—who are always a small minority of the community—no one pays much attention to their situation.

Given the burden of supporting an absolute stranger, the landlord's first reaction will be to try to transfer the subsidy to someone he knows better—a friend, a relative, or someone with whom he can barter or exchange favors. (Almost the entire Soviet economy, at the consumer level, works on the barter system.)

That is not how things work in an ordinary housing market. Under normal circumstances, a landlord's chief concern is finding people to rent his or her apartments. That is especially true of small investors who own only one or two buildings. To quote Anthony Downs once again:

> If a hundred units are operated by a hundred different owners, every vacancy represents a 100 percent loss of rental income. . . . Such owners try to avoid that outcome by raising rents cautiously. . . . This situation makes most small-scale landlords *turnover minimizers* rather than rent maximizers.

[1]Linda Matchan, "Wrestling with Rent Control: Brookline Candidates Talk of Animosity, 'Class Warfare,' " *Boston Globe*, May 6, 1991.

One way to minimize turnover is to find good tenants who will stay a long while, pay on time, and not damage the property. Most small owners give such tenants an incentive to remain by keeping their rents relatively low. As a result, long-term tenants typically have lower rents than short-term ones.[2]

Thus, the landlord's demands on tenants are usually simple— pay the rent on time, don't damage the property, and don't bother other tenants. (When sociologist Herbert Gans explored Boston's West End shortly before it underwent urban renewal, he found that landlords were disliked most for their insistence that tenants not bother other tenants. When the Boston Redevelopment Authority finally condemned the area and demolition was imminent, tenants held loud parties because "now we don't have to worry about bothering the landlord.")[3]

Under rent control, the dynamics are reversed. As the rents of long-standing tenants start to sink far below market levels, those tenants become a distinct liability. Most rent-controlled cities have some kind of vacancy allowance or vacancy decontrol, which subtly shifts the rental burden from older members of the community to newcomers and frequent movers. Whereas the differential between old tenants and new ones once represented the advantages of familiarity and reliability, long-term tenants are now a dead loss. Newcomers may well pay rents that are higher than market value. Where once a landlord feared vacancies, he now wishes for more.

As his rents are driven lower, a landlord must cut back on expenses. Mortgage payments (usually about 40 percent of a landlord's disbursements) are not easy to cut. Property taxes cannot be reduced (although the landlord may appeal his assessment on the grounds of reduced income). He can cut his profits, but competition has probably kept them to a minimum anyway. What he can do is start cutting down on maintenance.

The landlord begins to defer maintenance. He starts by cutting back on all the little things he used to do to attract tenants and keep them happy. The owner of a Berkeley housewares shop notes that,

[2]Anthony Downs, *Residential Rent Controls: An Evaluation* (Washington: Urban Land Institute, 1988), p. 35 (italics in original).

[3]Herbert Gans, *The Urban Villagers* (Glencoe, Ill.: Free Press, 1961).

since rent control, she no longer sees landlords in her store. "They used to be in here all the time buying curtains, window shades, all kinds of things. Now they say, 'If the tenants want those things, they can buy them themselves.' "[4]

So, gradually the apartment begins to become seedy. Rooms are no longer painted, hallways aren't kept clean, lightbulbs aren't replaced. Even larger problems may go untended. Plumbing is ignored, water leaks are left unrepaired, broken locks go unmended. "If you don't like it, why don't you move?" the landlord will say when tenants complain.

The truth finally hits the landlord. All his previous instincts were wrong. He used to worry about maintaining the place so he could attract good tenants and keep them. Now his best strategy is to get rid of tenants. And strangely enough, letting the place run down is the best way to do that.

Of course, the neglect does not go unnoticed by tenants or city hall. Tenant groups begin trooping to city council meetings to report that rent control isn't working. Landlords are refusing to maintain their properties. In fact, they are deliberately trying to make them uninhabitable in hopes of driving out tenants, thereby creating vacant units for which they can charge more rent. The city council must do something.

Anti-eviction laws soon go on the books. Code enforcement is strengthened. It is not long before someone comes up with an even better idea: why not let tenants themselves enforce the building code by allowing them to refuse to pay rent if there are code violations? The idea seems to make perfect sense. After all, landlords don't care about their buildings anymore, but tenants do. Why not give tenants responsibility for making sure their buildings are maintained?

So rent witholding for housing-code violations is legalized, and the next stage begins—something often called "the violations game." Tenants comb their buildings for the most trivial violations, hoping to save rent. There are always some to be found. If not, tenants can always create a few. A broken hall window, a few missing lightbulbs, a smoke alarm that has disappeared—all may be worth several months' rent.

[4]Interview with author.

40

Code violations become an easy rationale for not paying rent—especially for people who usually have trouble paying rent anyway. When New York City tenants go to housing court to answer eviction notices, they are routinely handed a form asking them to check off repairs that need to be made in their buildings. In Berkeley the rent board sends a form letter to tenants who have received eviction notices, stating: "Even if you have not paid the rent, you may have defenses you do not know about. For example . . . : Your rental unit *or any other rental unit on the property* is in substantial need of repair" (emphasis added).

It soon becomes impossible to evict anyone under any circumstances. Nonpayment of rent, doing damage to the property, bothering the neighbors—none of those things matter anymore. Now the guy on the third floor can blast his stereo all night and day with the supreme conviction that nobody can do a thing about it.

In 1989 the *San Francisco Examiner* carried the story of a woman who had rented an apartment to two young women on condition that there be no dogs and no more than three tenants. Two months later, she discovered that the apartment was being occupied by 10 people, 1 dog, and 2 cats. The apartment was a pigsty. Yet it took her five months and $4,000 to get the tenants evicted. A friendly law student helped the tenants delay the court proceedings for months. In the middle of the delays, the tenants even installed cable television. When they finally left, owing five months' rent, the stench in the apartment was so bad that the sheriff's department would not let the place be cleared until it had been checked for dead bodies.[5]

Another result of rent control is crack houses. Most landlords are terrified by the possibility of having drug dealers established in their apartments. "The first time I heard there was a dealer in my building, I went down there and ran him out with a baseball bat," says Aeolus Green, a Harlem landlord who owns two small buildings. "You can't imagine how fast drug dealers can ruin a building. They steal from your tenants; they scare people to death. You won't collect any rent for years if you let drug dealers get established."[6]

[5]Marsha Ginsburg, "A Landlord's Tale of Filthy Tenants," *San Francisco Examiner*, August 11, 1989.

[6]Interview with author.

Yet under blanket anti-eviction laws, drug dealers are given the same immunity as everyone else. In New York City, housing officials have required that alleged drug dealers have two drug convictions in the same year before they can be evicted. The city has been particularly reluctant to evict tenants from its own buildings—thereby setting a bad example for landlords. As a result, city-owned buildings are widely known as the best place to set up a drug business.

The way the system really works is indicated by another report from Berkeley. In 1989 the *San Francisco Examiner* reported that neighbors of a notorious crack house had won a landmark victory. Letters were pouring in from around the nation from homeowners trying to score a similar victory in their neighborhoods. As the story progressed, however, it became clear what this "victory" entailed:

> The Francisco Street solution was simple: Eighteen residents in June filed separate but consolidated suits in small claims court, charging the landlord with responsibility for cleaning up the drug activity that had made life in their quiet North Berkeley neighborhood a nightmare. . . .
> Berkeley-Albany Municipal Court Judge Jennie Rhine . . . ordered landlord Percy Davis to pay each of the 18 claimants $1,000 plus court costs for allowing activity "injurious to health" to continue on his property.[7]

No drug dealing had been curtailed. The building had not been cleaned up. All that had happened was that the landlord—a mechanic who lived about 20 blocks away—was hit for more money. At best, he could now initiate laborious eviction proceedings that would probably take months, cost thousands of dollars, and might not work anyway. Meanwhile, he was out another $18,000. That is the municipal equivalent of mugging. First, the landlord is slugged and kicked by municipal officials. Then, while he is lying unconscious, the public rifles his wallet.

And so it goes. Sooner or later, the landlord realizes that his investment is lost. Since everyone else is looting his building, he might as well grab what he can himself. He makes no repairs, stops paying the mortgage and property taxes, and just collects what

[7]Amy Alexander, "Tenants' Victory No Small Claim," *San Francisco Examiner*, August 31, 1989, p. A-14.

rents he can. He can probably pull out $20,000 to $30,000 before the building collapses. If he doesn't have the stomach for that, he can sell to a "slumlord" who does.

Collecting on fire insurance is another option. In New York City, landlord arsons became so common in some areas that the city responded with special welfare allowances. For a while, burned-out tenants were moved to the top of the list for coveted public housing. That gave *tenants* an incentive to burn down their buildings. They did, often moving television sets and furniture out onto the sidewalk before starting the fire. The South Bronx is the result.

Of course, the worst aspects of the war between tenants and landlords are generally reserved to the poorest neighborhoods, but the principle remains the same everywhere. In Santa Monica, fistfights have occurred between repairmen trying to fix rent-impairing violations and tenants who would prefer to keep the violations unrepaired so they don't have to pay rent. "We've had to call the police many times," says Al Markevicins, who manages several hundred apartments in Santa Monica.[8]

The ultimate victims are not landlords or tenants but a city's housing stock. Forced to lose money, landlords will eventually find ways to withdraw their property from the market, or they will allow their property to deteriorate until it is worth only what tenants are paying for it. But that only prompts tenants to pay less or withhold rent, which leads further down the road of deterioration.

Since the poor are most dependent on rental housing, they are the ultimate victims of the housing crisis.

[8]Interview with author.

6. Only in New York

I recently moved to New York from Texas and I pay $1,000 a month for a nice little apartment on the Lower East Side. The landlords have been reasonable, and the building is clean. Still, when I found out at a tenants' meeting that 30 of the building's 34 apartments rent below $200 and that most of the tenants in those cheap apartments make more money than I do, I was a bit outraged. I understand protecting the old people, but protecting fellow yuppies with bargains?

In Texas, $300 will pay rent on a two-bedroom apartment with air conditioning, washer/dryer, swimming pool, fireplace, and garage. The vacancy rate is over 20 percent. There are no rent controls, and tenants hold all the cards. And landlords are not a hated breed. If New Yorkers are so smart, why can't they see that what exists now is more than unfair? It's stupid.

—Letter to the
New York Daily News

The strange thing is that few New Yorkers believe that the housing situation can be any different. After more than 45 years of rent control, people in New York City honestly believe that finding an apartment is something akin to planning the Normandy invasion. They believe that if a landlord is forced to give up two years' back rent because a light fixture doesn't work, tenants everywhere have won a great victory. Yet they also believe that "big landlords run New York." Why else would there be such a housing shortage?

Believe it or not, it wasn't always like that. Once upon a time, New York was known as a city of nomads. There was so much housing available that people often had trouble putting down roots. Old-timers can remember the 1920s and 1930s when families would move every year just to get a new paint job. During the Depression, vacancy rates in New York ran close to 15 percent, and by 1940 they were still above 10 percent. In the late 1930s a group of realtors and civic leaders formed the "Live in Manhattan" society to encourage people to abandon the quiet life of the suburbs and fill the vacant apartments that abounded in the city.

Every autumn Manhattan would gear up for what was known as the fall renting season. Most affluent New Yorkers spent their summers at the beach or somewhere in the country. Housing was so plentiful that they would put their furniture in storage for three months to avoid paying rent. When they returned in September, they would find a new apartment. Eager landlords spent the entire summer making major repairs and sprucing up their buildings to attract new tenants when the fall matchmaking season began.

The reason for the superabundance of housing was that New York City—like the rest of the country—had very little housing regulation. Zoning had been invented in Manhattan in 1915. It was eagerly embraced by midtown and Park Avenue residents who were anxious to keep the garment district from spreading into their neighborhoods. Edgar Bassett, a Manhattan attorney, became the apostle of zoning and spread its gospel throughout the country.

But if New Yorkers were wary of industrial and commercial incursions, they had no compunctions about residences. During the 1920s builders put up an awesome amount of housing. Three times during the 1920s, more than 100,000 new units went up in one year. (Today, a year's output rarely goes over 10,000 units.) Almost every street of Upper Manhattan, the Bronx, and Brooklyn was filled with solid, four- and five-story walk-up buildings made of sturdy brick with beautiful stone facades.

The Depression brought a halt to building activity. Surprisingly though, it did not produce housing shortages. In fact, just the opposite occurred. There were large numbers of vacancies everywhere. People doubled up, and young couples postponed marriage in an effort to save money. Landlords, faced with falling rents and vacant apartments, trooped to the banks to try to renegotiate their mortgages.

Although money was tight, tenants who had resources still faced a buyer's market. On Park Avenue, several large new luxury buildings were marketed as the city's first cooperatively owned apartments. The market proved so soft that the developers were forced to withdraw the offer and rent the apartments at bargain prices. (When rent control was imposed, those embassy-sized apartments became the heirlooms of affluent families, passed on from generation to generation at the same low rents.)

Such was the situation when World War II began. The common memory is that the war produced intense housing shortages and that wartime rent controls were necessary to prevent gouging by greedy landlords. That is not entirely true for the rest of the country and certainly not true for New York City. In fact, New York was the last city in the country to be brought under federal wartime rent control.

Most goods and services were put under federal price controls in 1942 to allow the government to buy raw materials at normal price levels rather than bid against consumers in the regular economy. The price controls produced inevitable shortages, but rationing stamps were issued to distribute the burden evenly.

Although the government appropriated most building materials, it did not have any immediate need for rental housing. What made rent control necessary was the build-up of defense industries. Factory workers began flooding into cities such as Detroit, Chicago, and Los Angeles to fill the new jobs. Because they were well paid, defense workers could often outbid existing tenants for their apartments. To protect existing tenants in burgeoning defense cities—and avoid resentment against wartime workers—the government imposed rent control.

But that was not the case in New York City. Without any major defense industries, New York actually experienced an out-migration of almost a million people at the start of the war. Housing was so plentiful that in 1942 a group of civic leaders made a special plea to the Roosevelt administration to move several federal agencies to New York to relieve the housing shortage caused by bureaucrats flooding into Washington.

By 1943, in the midst of the war, New York City still had a vacancy rate of 8 percent. There were spot shortages in Brooklyn and Staten Island, where there were large Navy bases, but in the city as a whole, rents had barely risen since 1940. A voluntary campaign by landlords to keep rents reasonable was largely successful.

Nevertheless, there was tremendous agitation for rent control among New York's many tenant organizations. Mayor Fiorello La Guardia led the clamor. At one point in July 1943 he announced that Washington had assured him that rent controls would be imposed by the end of the month. Instead, the Office of Price Administration (OPA) issued an embarrassing rebuttal saying that there was still plenty of housing available in the city.

Finally though, the wartime freeze on all new construction took its toll. Vacancies crept down to 3 percent, and the voluntary program began to crack. One Queens apartment complex was reported to be evicting people because the landlord was under the impression that he could raise the rent for new tenants without violating the voluntary program.

On September 29, 1943, two days before New York's traditional "Moving Day" (when fall leases expired), Chester Bowles, director of the OPA, announced that New York would become the last city in the country to come under rent control. "We have found it necessary to take this step in spite of the remarkable record of those New York landlords . . . in holding down rents on a voluntary basis," said Bowles.[1]

New York City's housing crisis dates from that day. Since November 1943, New York has never been without rent control. Tenant organizations, always strong in New York, lobbied to have the controls continued by the state government after the federal program was discontinued in 1950. Administration of rent control has since bounced back and forth between the city and the state several times. Things have gotten so complicated that New York City now has two forms of rent control—the old controls dating from 1943 and a newer "rent stabilization" program, which was instituted in 1969. As a result, there are now three housing markets in New York City—rent-controlled units, rent-stabilized units, and the unregulated sector.

A rent-controlled apartment is the holy grail for New York's housing-starved populace. Most rent-controlled apartments are occupied by people who have been in continuous residence since 1971—and some have been occupied by the same people (or their friends or relatives) since 1943. Consequently, those units usually belong to "old New Yorkers"—people who were well established in the city during a previous generation.

People like Mia Farrow and Carly Simon (both from old New York families) have rent-controlled apartments. So do A. Whitney Ellsworth, publishing consultant to the *New York Review of Books*; James Levine, musical director of the Metropolitan Opera; William

[1]"OPA Orders Rents Frozen Here on March 1 Level Starting Nov. 1," *New York Times*, September 28, 1943.

Shawn, former editor of the *New Yorker;* Alistair Cooke; Philippe de Montebello, director of the Metropolitan Museum of Art; Theodore Sorensen, President Kennedy's one-time speechwriter; Suzanne Farrell, principal dancer with the New York City Ballet; state Sen. Manfred Ohrenstein (a vocal supporter of rent regulations); and former mayor Edward Koch. Rent-controlled tenants usually pay from 50 to 90 percent below market. There are about 155,000 rent-controlled apartments left in New York City, or 8 percent of the 1.9 million rental units.

Tenants of rent-controlled units do indeed have low median incomes ($10,800), and 24 percent are below the poverty line (the city average). But that is mainly because a majority of those tenants are retired. Their median age is over 65, and most are living in apartments that are far too large for them. New York is the only place in the country that averages fewer than two people per apartment. In 1988 Arthur D. Little, Inc., found that there were 175,000 apartments in New York in which one person occupied four or more rooms.[2]

Rent stabilization, imposed in 1969, is the newer form of rent control. Conceived by the administration of John V. Lindsay, it was supposed to avoid the problems of the old rent control—which had allowed only one rent increase in 25 years. Under rent stabilization, landlords are allowed annual rent increases at a rate determined by the Rent Stabilization Board. Every June thousands of tenants and landlords crowd into the board's hearings at One Police Plaza, waving placards and shouting insults at each other in a routine that has become so boring and predictable that even the newspapers don't cover it much anymore.

There are 900,000 rent-stabilized apartments. Most tenants probably pay from 10 to 40 percent below market, but as all rents march upward in lock step each year, some tenants of stabilized units are actually paying rents that are above market. In the poorer sections of the city, landlords often complain that they can't get anyone to pay the "legal" rents.

Finally, there are the 550,000 apartments—30 percent of the market—that for one reason or another are unregulated. Some are older

[2]Arthur D. Little, Inc., "Housing Gridlock in New York" (Arthur D. Little, Cambridge, Mass., 1988), p. 3.

49

apartments in small buildings (five units or less) that are exempt from rent stabilization. Some are in post-1974 buildings whose landlords have elected to stay outside rent stabilization. (The system is still voluntary for new construction.) Rented condominium units are one of the most common types of unregulated housing in New York. Rental income from individual apartments is so great that many condominium governing boards are now demanding a cut of the profits.

Virtually all tenants in the unregulated sector are now paying above-market prices because unregulated apartments are the only units that ever come on the market. Rent-controlled apartments are inevitably passed on to close relatives or sold for "key money" (prices begin at $10,000 and go as high as $150,000). Rent-stabilized apartments—although they occasionally appear in the newspaper listings—are usually sublet or passed on to friends and relatives.

As a result, anyone hunting an apartment in New York City has to look in the unregulated sector. The demand drives those prices sky high, leading to the universal impression that housing in the city is unaffordable. Yet the *median* rent in New York is only $390 a month—almost exactly what it is in Chicago and lower than in a dozen other major cities. The difference is that in New York City more than half the market is occupied by protected tenants who never move. As a result, people looking for apartments today must pay prices that are probably 20 to 50 percent higher than they would be without rent control.

On a single Sunday in March 1988, the *New York Times* ran 2,600 apartment ads, most of them for units in the upscale portions of the city. The average price of an apartment listed was $1,250—more than three times the city's median. Only one apartment—a small studio in Queens—was below the citywide median of $390.

On the same day, the *Chicago Tribune* listed 1,300 apartments for rent, mostly in upscale city neighborhoods. (Chicago's population is only one-third New York's.) The average rent was $650 a month, and 15 percent of all listings were below the citywide median of $380.

For just a small indication of what the housing situation does to New York City's social fabric, we need only look at the theater industry. In 1988 national entertainment columnist Roger Ebert reported that New York's Off-Off-Broadway theater industry was

50

being strangled because young actors and actresses coming to New York could no longer find places to live. The *Daily News* ran a similar story entitled "Next Stop, Pittsburgh," reporting that small theater groups were leaving New York because the players could no longer find housing. Yet at the same time, rent control was subsidizing such fading stars of the 1940s and 1950s as Van Johnson, Shelley Winters, Farley Granger, Barbara Bel Geddes, and Joyce Randolph. All had cheap, regulated apartments, many of which were used for only small portions of the year.

From New York City to Berkeley, the pattern is the same. Rent control rewards old-timers and punishes newcomers. Yet because newcomers are politically disorganized and rarely understand the system, they do not object to rent control and often demand that the system be more strictly enforced. As a result, the housing crisis constantly gets worse.

7. Disenfranchising the Poor

The preceding chapter has given an idea of what rent control does to people who are fairly affluent. But what about the people at the bottom of the income scale? How does rent control affect them?

The statistics on homelessness, of course, tell the story. New York City has the most elaborate shelter system in the country, the result of the 1979 lawsuit, *Callahan v. Carey*, which stipulated that the New York State constitution guarantees a "right to housing." (Only men were given the right. Women did not receive it until a subsequent lawsuit in 1982.)

On an average night in the winter of 1988–89, there were 6,000 men in New York City's shelters. At the same time, 12,000 homeless women and children were being temporarily housed in more than 100 welfare hotels around the city (at a cost of $36,000 a year for each family). If we use the conservative estimate that for each homeless person in the shelters there is at least one other in the streets, there were close to 40,000 homeless people in New York on any given night—a population almost twice the size of the city's police force.

All homelessness, of course, cannot be attributed to the shortage of suitable housing. In *Down and Out in America*, Peter Rossi, a professor of sociology at the University of Massachusetts, gives an excellent profile of the homeless and how they differ from other poor people. Comparing the homeless with recipients of General Assistance, the state-funded welfare program available to the extremely poor, Rossi found that, in general, homeless people had far more experience with drugs, alcohol, mental institutions, and the criminal justice system. Recipients of General Assistance, on the other hand—although often very poor or unemployed—seemed to be able to rely more on relatives and friends for shelter.

"Before becoming homeless," Rossi concluded, "it appears that, like the current General Assistance clients, [the homeless] managed to stay in homes mainly through the generosity of family and perhaps friends, supplemented by casual employment that did not qualify as a 'steady job.' Apparently such generosity has limits."[1] Nevertheless, Rossi concluded, housing does make a difference.

> The Chicago homeless families apparently have better prospects than homeless families in other cities. In contrast, the more than 3,000 New York City homeless families currently being housed in welfare hotels have dismal prospects, reflecting the much more meager supply of low-rent housing in New York.[2]

In the winter of 1988, I served as an informal guide through a Harlem homeless shelter for a young *Time* magazine reporter who had been assigned to do a story on the homeless. The reporter's editors—like many experts around the country—had decided that homelessness was being caused by gentrification, the renovation of decaying urban neighborhoods by middle-class people.

The men we visited were actually among the more self-possessed of the homeless, since the shelter was an elite institution, training them for jobs and personal responsibility. As a loyal reporter, my companion kept posing the question: "In your neighborhood have you seen middle-class people come in, buy a building, and make the tenants move out so they could fix it up for themselves?" The half-dozen men sitting around the table with us—all blacks in their 20s and 30s—shook their heads, no.

"Have you ever seen a case where a landlord up here in Harlem took a building and tried to fix it up so rich people could live in it?"

"Most of the buildings on my block are all boarded up," said one man.

"Well, then, what made you homeless?"

"I was living with my sister and we had a fire and after that I couldn't find any place to live," said one.

"I got strung out on dope and my mother kicked me out," said another.

"But haven't you found that rents have been pushed so high that you can't pay them anymore?" insisted the reporter.

[1]Peter H. Rossi, *Down and Out in America: The Origins of Homelessness* (Chicago: University of Chicago Press, 1989), p. 116.

[2]Ibid., p. 134.

54

"Paying rent's the least of my worries," said a third man. "You got to get yourself together and find a place; that's the big problem."

It is obviously wrong to argue that homelessness is purely a housing problem. The men we encountered at the Harlem shelter had many personal problems that had made them unstable and unproductive members of society. Yet the enormous problem of availability of housing in a city where vacancies have not risen above 3 percent in two decades clearly affected their social dysfunctioning. The homeless in New York City are not any different from the homeless in Houston or New Orleans. They just have far less housing available to them.

All that would be dismal enough, but what truly confounds most New Yorkers is that while 40,000 people in New York are homeless, the city itself holds title to 50,000 vacant apartments.

Those 50,000 vacant apartments are a source of general bewilderment that often gives rise to the kind of rumors heard in wartime. At one time there were reported to be vast plots afoot to clear Harlem and sell it to Donald Trump. The city is rumored to be in league with speculators everywhere. The fear of private enterprise in New York is so great that many community-planning boards actually oppose the city government's occasional efforts to sell a few buildings to private owners who want to fix them up, claiming such renovations will only drive up the price of housing in their neighborhoods.

In 1983 the city's Department of Housing Preservation and Development, which administers the vacant buildings, finally decided to put a good face on things. In a widely advertised effort, HPD started sealing the windows of vacant buildings with vinyl decals painted with pictures of pretty curtains and flowerpots. The object was to make it appear that the buildings were inhabited. "Appearance is reality," said former HPD commissioner Anthony Gliedman.

One obvious reason the city government has inherited so many vacant buildings is that rent control has driven so many landlords out of business. From 1975 to 1985, landlords walked away from 300,000 apartment units—enough to house comfortably the entire city of Buffalo. (Most landlords will even dispute the notion that landlords "walk away" from anything. "Every one of those buildings was torn from some landlord's bleeding hands," said Elizabeth

Ivory Greene, director of the Small Property Owners' Action Network.)[3]

The idea that the city government simply inherits abandoned buildings—usually taken in rem for taxes—is no longer accurate. The city government itself has become an active participant in confiscating property from private ownership. The procedure has become so formalized that it is fair to say that the city government is out hunting buildings for public takeover. Once the landlord has been driven off the property, the city government turns the property over to one of the dozens of government-funded neighborhood preservation companies that are becoming the major players in New York's low-income housing market.

To put it bluntly, New York City officials—with the enthusiastic support of the public—have decided that private ownership is the root cause of New York's shortage of low-income housing. Community ownership is to be the solution.

Since the 1970s the city government has sponsored a number of neighborhood preservation companies (NPCs) around New York City. Those groups are supposed to help organize the community for a variety of civic purposes—patrolling for crime, cleaning up vacant lots, assisting the elderly. The NPCs regularly receive large grants from major corporations such as Chase Manhattan, Citibank, and Con Edison. They also receive regular annual donations from HPD, the state government, and occasionally even the U.S. Department of Housing and Urban Development. In 1990 HPD's contribution to the NPCs was $12 million.

Although the NPCs regularly participate in community activities, their main efforts have been concentrated on housing. They organize rent strikes, hold tenant clinics, and even advertise for tenant organizers in the many small newspapers in New York dedicated to the housing problem.

Since the 1970s the city government has expressed a growing concern that rental housing has been falling into the hands of ever more unsophisticated investors, who are supposedly incapable of handling the job. In fact, the landlords of the 1970s were probably not much different from the landlords of the 1920s. As rent control hurt those people more and more, however, city officials became

[3]Interview with author.

56

convinced that they were not competent to handle housing. Harold Schultz, deputy general counsel for HPD's Office of Property Management, stated the case bluntly in a 1986 interview. "If New York landlords are in trouble, it's their own fault," he said. "They can't add and subtract. Dealing with regulations is just part of being a landlord."[4]

Since the 1970s, with ever-increasing momentum, the city government's strategy for providing low-income housing has been to take rental properties out of the hands of small investors and put them into the hands of what is called alternative management— tenant organizations, community groups, and private owners, all hand-picked by city officials.

The main vehicle for transfer has been section 7A of the Real Property Action and Procedures Law. The 7A program is so revealing of the differential treatment given private and public ownership in New York City that it is worth examining at length.

A 7A management program begins when either two tenants in a building or the commissioner of HPD asks a housing court judge to remove a building from the landlord's hands and place it in trusteeship under a court-appointed administrator. According to the statute, 7A action is justified if there is "a lack of heat or of running water or of light or of electricity or of adequate sewage disposal facilities, or any other condition dangerous to life, health, or safety, which has existed for five days." The 7A administrator is given authority to collect the rents and use the money to make major repairs on the building. Meanwhile, the landlord is not allowed on the property, although he must continue making mortgage payments and paying property taxes if he ever hopes to get his building back.

In theory, the purpose of 7A is to get the building into the hands of the city while it is still salvageable. Once the city has foreclosed— which it does in 95 percent of all cases—the building is recycled into one of the alternative management programs.

Incredibly, when a building comes under alternative management, the first thing HPD does is "restructure" the rents, meaning raise them. That is done so that the tenant group or community corporation will be able to make the building's income cover its

4Interview with author.

expenses. HPD feels that the existing rents are usually not enough to meet expenses, *even though the alternative manager is not making mortgage payments or paying property taxes.* When asked how private landlords can be expected to meet a building's expenses on existing low rents, HPD officials usually reply that a landlord has access to other resources—public expression of the common theory that all landlords are rich.

Despite all the kid-gloves treatment, the 7A program has essentially turned into a license to steal. The 7A administrators—sometimes tenant leaders, sometimes housing activists, sometimes friends of the judges—have generally taken the rent money and run.

By 1986 stories of larceny emanating from the 7A program had become so well known that the city's Department of Investigation made a special inquiry. The DOI found the program in a complete shambles. "In 1983," the DOI reported, "the average rental income from 7A buildings was estimated at $50,000 a year. In that year, total rental income from [all] buildings was estimated at $20 million."[5]

Yet essentially nobody knew or cared what happened to the money. "The courts possess all the legal authority for the program," said the DOI, "but [have] no resources for supervising 7As, while HPD has the resources but no authority." In addition, "no procedures exist for screening 7As," and "community groups involved in recruiting or serving as 7As are not adequately evaluated for their past performance in managing buildings; this has created opportunities for abuse."[6]

When the DOI requested financial records from 23 of the 7A administrators, only 9 were able to produce bank statements showing where the rent money had been deposited. "We reviewed the nine cases in our sample in which the bank statements corresponded to the first or last day of the month or for which there were sufficient consecutive statements to make a definitive determination," reported DOI. "The records that met these criteria revealed that a total of $105,806 in rental income was collected in a 21-month period. However, the corresponding bank statements indicated

[5]Thomas McDonald and Judith Frost, "An Analysis of Corruption: Vulnerabilities in New York City's 7A Administration Program" (City of New York Department of Investigation, 1986), p. 5.

[6]Ibid.

that only $49,857 was deposited into the building accounts. This means that only 52 percent of the funds can be legitimately accounted for."[7]

In other words, almost half the rent money had disappeared. And that was in the minority of cases for which financial records were available.

What is most remarkable is that, when confronted with those findings, the HPD, which administers the program, was essentially indifferent. For example, the DOI was highly critical of the HPD's 7A Monitoring Unit, saying it wasn't monitoring anything. In response, the HPD changed the unit's name to the Community Action Tenant Assistance Unit and said it would assume no further monitoring responsibilities.

Most remarkably, when the DOI documented case after case in which 7A administrators had stolen money, failed to make repairs, and cheated tenants out of thousands of dollars, the HPD responded by blaming the tenants.

In one case, the DOI found that a 7A administrator had stolen $300,000 in rents and failed to make any repairs over almost two years. Case records showed that when tenants reported the situation to the HPD, they were dismissed as "chronic complainers." When confronted by the DOI, the HPD responded:

> This case study clearly illustrates the "real" world that the 7A Counseling and Assistance Unit frequently faces. . . . The primary objective of 7A was achieved in this case. A building that would otherwise have been abandoned and emptied was, in fact, stabilized and survived to *in rem* vesting. Clearly the tenants could not have been too dissatisfied with [the administrator] since had they chosen they could have, at any time, sought to substitute themselves in the 7A action and assume control of the court case. . . . By HPD's definition this building was not a failure but a success.[8]

In another case, the DOI revealed that the 7A administrator had collected $166,000 in rents but had provided no bank statements and accounted for his expenditures only through a series of bills later proved fraudulent. During his administration, tenants had

[7]Ibid., p. 19.
[8]Ibid., pp. 40–41.

had neither heat nor hot water, and their plight had been the subject of a story in the *Amsterdam News*. Yet the HPD's response to the DOI was as follows:

> This case study illustrates an overemphasis on the importance of the 7A Administrator and a failure to accord tenants their appropriate role in the 7A process. . . .
> HPD offered to install boilers if the tenants agreed to come up with a $40,000 downpayment on the $114,000 job. The tenants throughout the 7A Administration took the position that they would not make payment and that it was our obligation to install the boiler. As a result, no boilers were installed, while the building was under 7A and [the administrator] was never able to provide heat. . . . Clearly there was no point to replacing an administrator where the continuing refusal by the tenants to cooperate with either the 7A or the City was the cause of the administrator's inability to provide services.[9]

The pattern, of course, is familiar. It is the same thing that happens in communist countries when the state takes over free enterprise and declares a workers' paradise, then outlaws strikes and labor unions. The DOI investigation made it obvious that the HPD's main concern is not the welfare of tenants but *getting buildings out of private ownership and into government hands*. As the HPD's response explained, "If the result of bringing a court motion for discharge [of an administrator] is to leave a building without a manager who can work with the tenants or to return it to a landlord bent on harassing the tenants out of the building, then it would be inappropriate for HPD to seek the discharge of an administrator."[10]

In 1986 then-mayor Edward Koch announced a $5.1 billion, 10-year program to solve New York's critical housing shortage. By 1989, subway posters put up during the mayoral election campaign showed Koch himself offering anyone in New York City an apartment.

The long-range plan is to confiscate thousands of buildings and turn them over to community organizations, which will be given

[9]Ibid., p. 45.

[10]Ibid., attached response from Anthony Gliedman, commissioner of Department of Housing and Urban Development to Patrick W. McGinley, commissioner, Department of Investigation, December 13, 1985, p. 5.

hundreds of millions of tax dollars to rehabilitate them. Those community groups are intensely political, staffed by full-time activists with close ties to the various factions of the Democratic party. There have already been reports that community groups can deliver the votes of thousands of tenants in crucial primaries. Having driven thousands of landlords out of business through rent control, the city government now plans to become landlord to close to a million New Yorkers.

The New York experience shows where government housing regulation is ultimately headed. The pattern has recurred over and over. First the government regulates private enterprise, preventing it from supplying cheap and plentiful goods. Next, the government argues that the lack of cheap and plentiful goods proves private enterprise doesn't work. Government production must be substituted. To do that, the government must confiscate the means of production. Once the means of production are in government hands, however, the state becomes totally indifferent to the desires of consumers and tells people to shut up and be happy with what they have.

The horrifying thing about government confiscation of private housing is that not only do consumers suffer but upward mobility is destroyed. Howard Husock, of Harvard's Kennedy School of Government, has argued that the solution to the nation's housing problems is the three-decker flat—a detached home frequently built in American cities during the 1920s. The three-decker offered working-class people both cheap rental housing and the opportunity for homeownership. The symbiotic relationship between landlords and tenants produced upward mobility for all. Predictably, the three-decker was outlawed by zoning reformers of the 1920s. In its place, the affluent reformers offered public housing.[11]

It is now clear that public housing offers people neither better housing nor a more benign landlord. Instead, public housing becomes a trap, locking its residents into permanent dependency. Housing regulations, rent control, and the substitution of "affordable" government-subsidized housing are doing the same thing.

[11]Howard Husock, "Rediscovering the Three-Decker House," *Public Interest*, Winter 1990.

Tragically, the confiscation of private housing also destroys the chances of upward mobility for the most ambitious. In Harlem 70 percent of all residential property is now owned by the city of New York. An entire generation of working-class landlords has been wiped out by the city government's predatory housing policies. For both landlords and tenants, the government takeover of housing has meant increased dependency, downward mobility, and—ultimately—homelessness.

8. Beyond Public Housing

Rent control is the reason vacancy rates are so low and problems of homelessness so severe in the major cities where it is practiced— New York, Boston, Washington, San Francisco, and Los Angeles. But it does not explain homelessness in other cities, nor does it explain the problem of affordable housing in general. To understand that, we must look at the housing market as a whole.

One of the most tragic misunderstandings in the public arena occurs when people oppose new housing construction on the grounds that it will only benefit the rich and do nothing to provide housing for people with low to moderate incomes.

The first thing that must be recognized about housing is that, once built, it lasts a long, long time. Food is usually consumed within days or weeks of purchase. A good suit of clothes may last 5 to 10 years. The average car has a life expectancy of 11 years, and a major appliance will probably last about that long. But a new home, on the day it is first occupied, can be expected to last at least 75 years—decades longer than any other consumer item.

As a result, almost everybody lives in used housing. Only about 1 percent of the market each year is new housing, which is generally consumed by affluent people. The average buyer of a new home has an income of $60,000, compared with $40,000 for used-home buyers and only $15,000 for tenants.

Yet it is of little consequence that poor people cannot buy new homes. The important thing is that when affluent people move into a new home they leave an empty home behind. That unit is almost always occupied by someone less affluent. That person in turn leaves another home to someone who is still less affluent, and so on down the line. Housing rarely disappears from the market, except when it becomes completely dilapidated or outmoded. For that reason, new housing built for the affluent not only serves people at the top of the income scale, it affects people all the way down to the bottom end of the market. The effect is called "filtering."

One of the most influential books ever written about the housing market is a slim volume entitled *New Homes and Poor People*, a study of the filtering process written by John B. Lansing, Charles Wade Clifton, and James N. Morgan, all of the Institute for Social Research at the University of Michigan.[1] In 1966 the authors randomly picked 1,000 new homes built in 13 major cities during a three-month period the previous year. Contacting the new owners, the authors surveyed their income characteristics and then asked for the address they had just left. Going to that address, the researchers found the new resident and did the same thing. Each chain of moves was followed back until it ended—either with an unvacated unit (a young person who had just left his parents' home, for example) or a unit that was left permanently vacant.

The authors found that the average chain lasted about 3.5 moves. That meant that for the 1,000 new homes built, 3,500 other housing units were made available. Moreover, the chains quickly worked their way down into lower income brackets. For every three new homes built, one unit became available to a person living below the poverty line. Although most of the new homes were built in the suburbs, chains quickly worked their way back into central cities.

The conclusion was that filtration works. Housing built for the rich does not benefit just the rich. All housing is essentially part of one market. New housing built in one place will open opportunities in another. The only sluggishness the authors found was across racial lines. Blacks were underrepresented at every stage of the process. That seemed to be mainly the result of racial discrimination. In addition, chains involving blacks tended to end more quickly because blacks were often moving out of already over-crowded quarters and did not leave vacant units behind.

The dynamics of filtration make it clear why society gets the most effective return from money spent on housing that is built for the upper end of the market. The problem with housing built for the poor is that too often it turns out to be poor housing. When builders cut corners and scale down their projects to try to make them affordable, they usually end up producing something that will not last very long. As a result, it will not offer long-term service to

[1]John B. Lansing, Charles Wade Clifton, and James N. Morgan, *New Homes and Poor People* (Ann Arbor, Mich.: Institute for Social Research, 1969).

anyone, rich or poor. From the point of view of social efficiency, it makes more sense to build housing to the highest possible standards. That means building for the affluent.

On the other hand, it does not mean that cheap housing should not be built to meet people's immediate needs when the market will support it. Low-income housing can be extremely remedial in many situations.

Take mobile homes. Although few people realize it, mobile homes are the nation's prime form of low-income housing. Selling for about $20,000 a unit, mobile homes are bought by people who have an average income of only $18,000 a year. Moreover, people generally prefer them to other forms of low-income housing. A 1973 survey by architecture students at the University of Arkansas found that many mobile-home owners considered a single-family home ideal "but felt that they could not afford to buy one. . . . They could buy a good-quality mobile home for about the same monthly payment as they could rent an apartment."[2]

Except in the major cities and suburbs of the Northeast, mobile homes are an important mainstay of the nation's housing stock. From 1980 to 1985 mobile home placements in the South exceeded the total number of housing starts in the entire Northeast.[3] Many people have suggested that New York solve its problems by using the vast vacant areas of the South Bronx as trailer parks.

Suburbs and upsale communities vigorously zone out mobile homes—even when they would be owner occupied—because they are "tacky" and attract the wrong kind of people. Even the radical-dominated Santa Monica City Council turned down the recommendation of a citizens' advisory council on housing that mobile home parks be allowed in that affluent suburb of Los Angeles.[4]

Are mobile homes the answer to our low-income housing problems? Yes and no. In the short run, they obviously can help. To people who have spent their lives in wooden shacks in the rural South, mobile homes may seem the height of luxury. Loosening

---

[2]Mike Moose, ed., *The Immobile Home Syndrome* (Fayetteville: University of Arkansas, School of Architecture, 1973).

[3]James Hughes and George Sternlieb, "The Future of America's Housing" (Center for Urban Research, New Brunswick, N.J., 1986), p. 134.

[4]Michael Kann, *Middle Class Radicalism in Santa Monica* (Philadelphia: Temple University Press, 1984), p. 176.

zoning restrictions could do much to alleviate housing shortages in cities and suburbs. (Most municipalities that allow mobile homes today restrict them to industrial and commercial zones.)

In the long run, however, it probably makes sense to construct more permanent housing. Mobile homes have a life expectancy of only about 20 years. They decline steadily in value and offer their owners no capital appreciation—which is one reason they are relatively inexpensive.

The same holds true for public housing. Some of it can probably be justified on the grounds that there is simply no other housing available. But much of the impetus for public housing has come from people who believe that the government makes a better landlord.

Public housing was originally conceived as housing for the "submerged middle class" during the Depression. In many ways it was the successor to the "model tenements" run by reform groups during the 19th and early 20th centuries. Public housing projects were seen as schools for middle-class behavior. Early administrators prided themselves in 100 percent rent collection and often held classes to help residents "graduate" to homeownership.[5]

As the submerged middle class left for the suburbs, however, public housing projects gradually became the refuge of the poorest of the poor—particularly the black poor. Throughout the 1950s and 1960s, many housing authorities tried to maintain the old standards. Unmarried mothers were excluded, and families could be evicted if a son was a drug addict or a breadwinner was in prison.

The construction of high-rise projects in the 1950s and the increasing dissolution of black family life inevitably led to changes. In city after city, public housing projects "turned," that is, lost their few remaining white inhabitants (often the elderly) and became the pathology-ridden "vertical ghettos" of today.

Unfortunately, much public housing, built to low standards of construction, has not lasted. All over the country, cities are starting to tear down many of the large housing projects that were built in the 1950s and 1960s. The Pruitt-Igoe complex in St. Louis, dynamited in 1974, only 15 years after it won architectural awards for

---

[5]Lawrence M. Friedman, *The Government and Slum Housing: A Century of Frustration* (Chicago: Rand McNally, 1968), p. 139ff.

excellence, was the symbol of the process. During the 1980s, 12,856 of the nation's million public housing units were razed.

The Reagan administration was criticized for allegedly not spending money to maintain public housing projects, but that is not the case. Federal operating subsidies to public housing authorities increased from $755 million in 1980 to $1.4 billion in 1987. Modernization funds, used by the housing authorities for long-term maintenance, rose from $1 billion in 1980 to $2.6 billion in 1983, before eventually dropping again to $1.4 billion in 1988.

The commonly cited statistic that HUD's budget authorizations dropped from $30 billion in 1980 to $12 billion in 1987 is true but virtually meaningless. Authorizations are not spending. They are only commitments to spend money in the future. Actual federal spending on low-income housing rose from $5.7 billion in 1980 to $13.8 billion in 1988, a 50 percent increase after adjusting for inflation.

Since 1980 the Reagan and Bush administrations have been trying to get the government out of the expensive business of building and operating public housing. After studying the problem for two years, the President's Commission on Housing reaffirmed in 1982 what housing experts had been saying for over a decade—the availability of adequate housing units is no longer a real problem.[6] The massive explosion of suburban housing construction in the 1950s and 1960s essentially emptied the cities, leaving much older housing available. That housing was quickly occupied by the urban poor. Zoning and no-growth efforts have since slowed the process, but the old problem of substandard and dilapidated housing has essentially been overcome.

In 1950 one-third of all American households still lacked complete plumbing. Today the figure is 2 percent. In 1950 half of American homes were heated with coal or wood. Today the figure is 5 percent. As James Hughes and George Sternlieb of Rutgers University point out, there is now one bedroom for every American.[7]

The President's Commission concluded that the main problem for low-income tenants was income. Housing is available; some

[6]*The Report of the President's Commission on Housing* (Washington: Government Printing Office, 1982).

[7]Hughes and Sternlieb, p. 177.

people just can't afford it. Particularly with the rise of single-parent families among the poor, lack of income has become the principal impediment to securing decent housing.

As a result, the President's Commission proposed replacing the expensive, time-consuming business of constructing public housing with a system that would give financial assistance directly to tenants. Housing vouchers, which had been recommended for decades, were finally authorized in 1984 under section 8 of the Housing and Community Development Act of 1974.

The Carter administration—not entirely sold on the idea of tenant choice—had created section-8 housing "certificates" that were a kind of halfway step toward vouchers. Not wanting to let too much power slip out of the hands of the government, the administration set up an elaborate procedure whereby the government would help the poor choose housing and then pay the landlord. Those certificates were also issued for periods of 15 years, effectively immobilizing tenants and creating assured occupancy for landlords and developers.

In practice, the certificate program became a rehash of the old public housing system. Section-8 certificates were used both as the basis for programs of new construction and for "substantial" and "moderate" rehabilitation. The certificates were handed out in large blocs, virtually ensuring the success of any new or rehabilitated project. (The distribution of the moderate-rehabilitation certificates eventually became the crux of the scandals that rocked HUD in the late 1980s.)

When it took office in 1980, the Reagan administration immediately chopped away the new-construction program and cut back on the rehabilitation programs. It switched to a pure voucher program in 1984. Vouchers are provided to the tenant, rather than the landlord or developer. They allow low-income people to find housing wherever they wish. The vouchers are issued for 5 years, not 15, which increases their flexibility. The voucher program also cut future authorizations—which is what led to the false charges about huge spending cuts during the Reagan era. When a 15-year certificate is authorized, all 15 years' spending is credited to the first year. The switch to vouchers did not cut spending; it only shortened the time frame over which money is committed.

Most important, *vouchers allow more poor people to be served.* A voucher costs only about $4,000 a year, whereas a certificate costs

$6,000 (mainly in administrative overhead), and a unit of public housing costs $10,000. Thus, it is not surprising to find that, by 1989, *more poor people were being served by federal housing assistance than ever before.* Over 4.2 million low-income tenants were receiving federal housing assistance, compared with only 3.1 million in 1980.

Vouchers have also proved easier to target to the poorest of the poor. As the HUD scandals revealed, many of the section-8 certificates for new and rehabilitated housing ended up serving the middle class. That was not entirely due to corruption. The certificates were indeed very hard to target. Once in the hands of a landlord or a developer, a certificate might end up benefiting just about anyone. The advantage of vouchers is that they put the subsidy directly into the hands of the people whom they are intended to aid.

There is, however, one problem. Vouchers have proved to be all but unredeemable in cities with rent control. The logic is inexorable. In a market where hundreds of thousands of people are kept in place by below-market rents and developers are scared out of the market by rent regulations, even having enough money to spend on housing may not be sufficient.

Thus, in Boston 45 percent of the low-income people issued section-8 vouchers are returning them unused. Even with a $250-a-month federal supplement they cannot find housing in a city where the median rent is only $350. In New York City, things are worse. Over 60 percent of the vouchers have been returned unused.

New York City housing officials are so philosophically opposed to the idea of allowing federal money to be passed through to landlords that for many years they *refused to distribute any federal section-8 funds* on the grounds that they should be spent only on city-owned apartments. In 1987 New York was the only city in the nation that failed to spend its section-8 rent supplements. The reason was that it refused to allow the money to go to private landlords. That took place in the city with the nation's worst housing shortage and one of the most severe homeless problems.

The battle for affordable housing will not be won until we cut back on the power of municipalities to zone out affordable housing and persuade them to give up rent control. All the federal subsidies in the world will not be able to overcome the folly of a city that refuses to allow housing to be built, deliberately undermines its

own housing stock, and then tries to substitute government ownership of housing.

Housing is housing. The only way to have enough of it is to build
more of it. Building and preserving good housing stock are the keys
to solving the housing problem.

9. Conclusion

The common perception of the low-income housing shortage is that it is a national issue. In October 1989 more than 25,000 protesters descended on Washington to ask Congress and the Bush administration to take action to solve the housing problem.

Yet housing is not a truly national issue. The federal government has never played anything but a minor role in providing low-income housing, and that role has become less and less important as basic housing stocks have increased.

Housing problems are caused by municipal government. It is municipalities that practice the exclusionary zoning and growth moratoria that prevent cheap, multifamily housing from being built. It is municipalities that have initiated strict building-code enforcement campaigns that have often led to the closing of single-room-occupancy hotels and other affordable housing in the central cities. And it is municipalities that have imposed rent control, the quickest and most efficient way to produce a housing shortage.

Because housing so directly affects the local environment and because municipal governments now exercise so much regulatory authority over how much and what kind of housing is to be built, the American housing industry, which is easily capable of producing good housing for everyone, has been stymied. Any industry would suffer the same fate in the same regulatory environment. If General Motors had to go around the country negotiating with every little municipal planning board before it could sell automobiles in a town or city, we would have a "car shortage" as well.

The local nature of housing problems poses some difficulties for any administration that is trying to cut back on federal authority and revive state and local governments. No matter what kind of money is spent, municipal governments can perpetuate the problem through their own regulation.

Should the federal government, then, try to break down zoning barriers and abolish rent control at the national level? The temptation to do so is certainly great.

It is particularly appealing to try to overturn rent control and various growth restrictions in the courts. Rent control and growth restrictions represent such an obvious tyranny of the majority and seem so clearly in violation of the Fifth Amendment's prohibition against "taking private property for public purposes without just compensation" that it is hard to believe the courts will not eventually rule against them. It is hard to conceive of a clearer violation of property rights. Unless the Constitution is to become completely "gentrified"—protecting only people who work with their heads, not their hands—it seems inevitable that a suit against them will one day succeed.

Yet on the whole, I think I would argue against the tactic of running to the courts for rulings on every public issue.

It is no exaggeration to say that a court decision overturning local zoning or outlawing rent control in New York or San Francisco would probably meet with the kind of massive popular resistance that once accompanied school desegregation in the South. Our judicial system should not be afraid of such reactions, but it seems much wiser that such issues be thrashed out in public debate, both in Congress and in the state legislatures.

Every set of municipal housing restrictions is adopted by the majority with the intent of abridging the rights of small, hard-to-identify minorities. Zoning regulations discriminate against people who may want to move into a community in the future, not people who are already there. Rent control lowers rents for the vast majority of tenants but leaves a small, marginal group facing a housing shortage.

Those issues should be the concern of Congress and the state governments. We are still one vast "common market"—a country where, in theory at least, all people are free to live wherever they wish as long as they can afford it. Both zoning and rent control are political manipulations that prevent people from exercising their right to buy and sell in a free market.

The solution to the housing problem lies in letting the free market work. It lies in letting consumers have their choice. It lies in limiting the power of government and leaving the American people free to solve their own problems with their own creative energies.

About the Author

William Tucker is a contributing editor at *Forbes*. He has written for *Harper's*, the *New Republic*, the *Atlantic*, *National Review*, the *American Spectator*, the *New York Times*, the *Washington Post*, and the *Wall Street Journal*. He is the author of three previous books, *Progress and Privilege*, *Vigilante*, and *The Excluded Americans: Homelessness and Housing Policies*.

Cato Institute

Founded in 1977, the Cato Institute is a public policy research foundation dedicated to broadening the parameters of policy debate to allow consideration of more options that are consistent with the traditional American principles of limited government, individual liberty, and peace. To that end, the Institute strives to achieve greater involvement of the intelligent, concerned lay public in questions of policy and the proper role of government.

The Institute is named for *Cato's Letters*, libertarian pamphlets that were widely read in the American Colonies in the early 18th century and played a major role in laying the philosophical foundation for the American Revolution.

Despite the achievement of the nation's Founders, today virtually no aspect of life is free from government encroachment. A pervasive intolerance for individual rights is shown by government's arbitrary intrusions into private economic transactions and its disregard for civil liberties.

To counter that trend, the Cato Institute undertakes an extensive publications program that addresses the complete spectrum of policy issues. Books, monographs, and shorter studies are commissioned to examine the federal budget, Social Security, regulation, military spending, international trade, and myriad other issues. Major policy conferences are held throughout the year, from which papers are published thrice yearly in the *Cato Journal*. The Institute also publishes the quarterly magazine *Regulation* and produces a monthly audiotape series, "Perspectives on Policy."

In order to maintain its independence, the Cato Institute accepts no government funding. Contributions are received from foundations, corporations, and individuals, and other revenue is generated from the sale of publications. The Institute is a nonprofit, tax-exempt, educational foundation under Section 501(c)3 of the Internal Revenue Code.

CATO INSTITUTE
224 Second St., S.E.
Washington, D.C. 20003